D1345725

AYE READY

ALSO BY PAUL SMITH

Tannadice Idols

Shearer Wonderland (with Duncan Shearer)

Pittodrie Idols

AYE READY

RANGERS WAR HEROES

PAUL SMITH

BLACK & WHITE PUBLISHING

First published 2011
by Black & White Publishing Ltd
29 Ocean Drive, Edinburgh EH6 6JL

1 3 5 7 9 10 8 6 4 2   11 12 13 14

ISBN: 978 1 84502 353 9

A CIP catalogue record for this book is available from the British Library.

Typeset by Iolaire Typesetting, Newtonmore
Printed and bound by Scandbook AB

To Coral, Finlay, Mia and Zara – the dream team

CONTENTS

ACKNOWLEDGEMENTS

There can be no more complex or sensitive subject in British history than the First and Second World Wars. With that in mind, I owe a debt of gratitude to the veritable army of people who contributed advice in all measures along a fascinating journey. Colin MacLeod, with his attention to detail and tenacious spirit, once again provided vital support while Campbell Brown and his dedicated team at Black & White Publishing, from the initial idea to the finishing touches, were a driving force in the project. Editor Mike Murphy tackled his task with patience and diligence while contributions from family members of Rangers heroes, including Jean Cox, the devoted wife of Sammy Cox, and Walter Tull's surviving relatives Pat Justad and the Reverend Duncan Finlayson were hugely appreciated. Dave Pendleton, with his enthusiasm for the life and times of Jimmy Speirs, was enormously helpful and all were gracious enough to spare their time and memories to add a personal touch. There were professional contributions from Annabel Reeves and Paul Murray, amongst others, whilst the veterans' charity Erskine also lent its support along with the British Red Cross and its archive team. Derek Bird at the Western Front Association and many, many others at various regimental museums and military archives also had a part to play. Without each of them it would not have been possible to pull so many facets together. As always, the greatest thanks go to Coral, Finlay, Mia and our new baby Zara for the inspiration to get over the finish line once again at the end of a marathon effort.

INTRODUCTION

Too many games they cry, not enough rest. We need a winter break they plead, time to recharge the batteries and soak up the sun. The contract is too short, the pay packet not big enough. The media scrutiny is too intense, the supporters are far too demanding.

Ever since covering my first Scottish Premier Division football match in the mid-1990s, I have reported on all of those issues and more as our national game's many and varied woes have been placed under the microscope for close analysis at one stage or another.

For better or worse we have a tendency to take our national game, or perhaps national obsession, very seriously. Molehills can become mountains very quickly amid the furore whipped up around even the smallest of grumbles or complaints. From refereeing decisions to ticket prices, we have all become animated at some point or another by aspects of the sport that grab you by the lapels and won't let go.

And then it hits you; does any of it really matter? Probably not. If the stars of today are asked to play a few extra matches or to push themselves that little bit harder, what is the worst that can happen? A hamstring strain here, a shin splint there. Are the protracted contract negotiations of each and every summer something we should be getting exercised about? Careers in football are short but the rewards are, in the main, handsome. Is the glare of the press spotlight a price worth paying for the privileged lifestyle afforded to players at the top level? On balance, yes.

What puts the trials and tribulations of the current crop of players into a stark context is the type of adversity faced by their forebears during the two world wars. Those were the men who knew real struggle and who faced the challenges with a remarkable lack of drama. War became part and parcel of life for the men of both eras, and footballers, like every other section of society, had to knuckle down and lay their life on the line for their country. No questions asked, no excuses given. These were not superstars who had a fortune to fall back on, rather a different type of superstar, ordinary working men who happened to go to work at a football ground rather than a colliery or factory. They lived in ordinary houses on ordinary streets but were responsible for extraordinary acts. It is a humbling experience to look back on those times and note the sacrifices made. Some were lucky enough to return un-scathed, save for the mental scars inflicted by battle. Others were less fortunate and landed back on British soil bearing the physical injuries of war. Just as many did not return at all, paying the ultimate price for their nation's part in both the First World War and the Second World War. We have all watched from afar as today's troops do battle in Afghanistan and have listened as yet more names are added to the list of fatalities from that particular theatre of war. It is very difficult to imagine the prospect of waving off a clutch of current Ibrox idols ready to join the effort, yet that is exactly what Rangers supporters did on two occasions during the first half of the twentieth century. Picture Alan McGregor marching off in full combat gear with a machine gun over his shoulder or Ally McCoist getting to grips with a deadly Taliban explosive device. It sounds totally and utterly absurd, but that type of complete role reversal became terrifyingly normal for a generation of fans who would serve side by side in the trenches with the men they had once cheered from the terraces. There was no place for airs and graces on the part of the football fraternity and equally no time for their comrades to be star struck; just as in the Rangers dressing room, it was a case of one for all and all for one. Many Rangers men, either past or present during the war years, went on to win honours for their bravery in the field. Many Rangers men lost their lives. Others went about their business quietly and efficiently in all areas of the forces, home and abroad, and each and every one had a part to play. *Aye Ready* is about piecing together a football narrative with the more sombre story of the war, attempting to put in context the impact the conflicts had on a group of men who had once dreamt only of scoring goals and winning trophies but who quickly had to rewrite their career plan when the forces called. In the Great War there were characters such as Walter Tull and Jimmy Speirs leading the way on the frontline. Both were killed in action, both had in one way or another an Ibrox link and both could not have realised the way in which they would capture the imagination in England and Scotland long after falling on foreign soil.

Tull's story is a captivating one and perhaps the most documented of all of the Great War's football tales. Much has been made of his stock as a Tottenham and Northampton Town idol and little of his Rangers link. Mentioned fleetingly here and there, the challenge was to put flesh on the bones of the long-standing suggestion that the great man was a Gers man in waiting. What has emerged is that the connection was a definite one and that it extended far beyond a fleeting notion of wishing to play for Scotland's leading lights – there was a far more substantial pull towards Ibrox than that, a strong family bond to the club. Anecdotal evidence suggests the heroic Tull did play in light blue during the war years but, more poignantly, it is clear that had he not been killed in action he would have been bound for a settled and, it is fair to assume, successful career at Ibrox. What is little known is that Tull's Scottish connection remains strong to this day. Indeed, he is at the centre of an ongoing tartan mystery as efforts continue to trace the wartime mementoes that vanished from their resting place north of the border in relatively recent times.

During the course of researching this project I have been fortunate to speak to members of his surviving family, based in the Highlands, and gleaned not only fascinating insights into the life and times of their famous ancestor, but also a feel for the pride that still burns strong within those who share a blood line with the war hero.

He harboured dreams of finally laying his hat in Glasgow, near to his brother and sister, but never had that opportunity – just as he never had the opportunity to finalise his move to Rangers. It is a tragic story, peppered with moments of triumph and high in achievement, and one well worth recounting for a Rangers audience.

The warmth Tull's family express towards his memory is mirrored in England, where Jimmy Speirs is the object of affection for a group of dedicated supporters who have worked tirelessly to make a new generation aware of his exploits as a soldier and football player. Speirs was a former Rangers player when he was killed in action, but his Ibrox connection is strong after an extended spell in the first team before his career took him south to Bradford. Through speaking to those who have revisited the grave of the heroic Scotsman, it has become clear that the efforts of the brave men who fought under the union flag continue to reverberate long after the battlefields fell silent.

They died in a very different time from the one we know now

as football fans. They were not made rich by the game they loved, but they did leave behind a treasure trove of memories and life stories that tug at the heart in a way the modern soap opera of professional sport simply cannot.

Tull and Speirs have become well-known national symbols of the First World War and its impact on sport, while the likes of Finlay Speedie have grown to take on greater significance closer to home through achievements in a Rangers jersey coupled with gallantry in army uniform. All went through incredible hardships while serving king and country, discovering that past glories counted for very little in the heat of battle.

In the Second World War the technology had advanced but the principles remained very much the same. Selflessness was the order of the day as player after player signed up to put life and limb in jeopardy while wearing British colours in every conflict from Africa to Southern Italy and Northern France. Wherever there was a battle, it appears there was a Rangers contribution.

In the Royal Air Force and Royal Navy there were prominent Ibrox figures engaged to varying degrees, whether dodging German anti-aircraft fire in daring raids or putting their fitness expertise to good use in training the men tasked with tackling Hitler's forces.

In the army there were those recognised for extreme acts of bravery, including the legendary Willie Thornton for his exploits in one of the most audacious British movements of the Second World War. Specialists were also pressed into action, including among the Royal Army Medical Corps tending to the casualties in all corners of the world.

It was not all doom and gloom, with football called upon to provide rare moments of light relief during that period. Highlights included a record-breaking Old Firm effort by the players assembled by Bill Struth, often at short notice, during the wartime competitions as well as cameo appearances from some world stars during the whirlwind procession of guest players on all sides, in what at times was a surreal period for the game. Throughout it all, the beautiful game had a beautiful habit of bringing smiles back to faces that had otherwise worn frowns.

Given many more years and limitless resource it would perhaps be possible to piece together every last detail of every Ranger ever to serve. Without those benefits it is at least possible to put together a snapshot of what the war years meant to the club and its players, with the aid of the records that have survived and that are available in various archives and re-sources. Occasional first-hand accounts have sprung up, either from players themselves or those who worked side by side with the household names who were pressed into action. The major regret is that the vast majority of men who did their country proud are no longer with us to recount their own story, with so many long since departed.

How fantastic it would have been to sit down with Willie Thornton and hear his account of the act that won him his Military Medal. It would have been an education to chew the fat with Ian McPherson and listen intently to the detail of the first bombing raids he flew over enemy territory as one of the RAF's leading lights.

Unfortunately that was not a privilege I could enjoy, but through researching the campaigns these men were involved in there is a feel for just what they encountered along the way and a huge respect for the way in which they were able to embrace their new role as men of war.

Among the very few survivors is the hugely popular char-acter Sammy Cox, now retired and living a peaceful life in the leafy suburbs of North America, having moved across the Atlantic during the final years of his playing career. I benefited greatly from the assistance of Cox's wife Jean, who revealed a long-lasting tribute that she and her illustrious husband made to mark his army career.

What the story of Cox demonstrates is that soldiers did not have to be exposed to the horrors of the frontline to be touched by service. His role was back at base on Scottish soil, helping to train his fellow army recruits, and it was all part of the huge effort at home and abroad to defeat the German forces. Everyone had a part to play and did so with pride and dedication; it was one army with one common goal and a sense of purpose.

The war cut through the early years of the football career of Cox, although like so many of his fellow soldiers he was able to keep himself in shape during regular run-outs for club and select teams. Indeed, the benefits of army football became clear to the Rangers legend in later years when he used his experiences to help Scotland's cause against the Auld Enemy. These little gems are all part of the tapestry that came together during the war years, glimmers of lighter moments that rose from grim times.

As Jean Cox herself noted, too many of her husband's peers are sadly no longer with us. Willie Thornton was among those who played alongside Cox in the great Rangers sides of the post-war years, helping to bring a sense of enjoyment back to a city after the austerity of war. There was a new freedom in society and that was reflected in all sectors of entertainment, not least football. For Thornton to have returned from battle in Italy, where his gallantry saw him honoured, and slot back into life as an Ibrox star is testament to his character. He had grown used to hero status on the field and showed the same qualities while in an army uniform rather than football kit.

Thornton's experiences, first in Africa and then on the very fringes of Europe in Sicily, show just how far reaching the Scottish effort was during the Second World War. In every war-torn land, there was influence from the Scots as part of the victorious British effort, and the contrasts between the operations in different corners of the globe were a major part of the jigsaw that slotted together to keep the Nazis at bay.

Men such as Thornton, a truly gentle soul who was far more at home in among the soil of his garden than the mud of the trenches, were forced to take on very different characteristics and did so without question. Their country needed them and they were ready to serve, Aye Ready in fact.

While the bulk of *Aye Ready* is dedicated to the Great War and the Second World War experiences, it would have been remiss not to at least touch on later campaigns that impacted upon the Ibrox favourites Harold Davis and Jock Wallace. Indeed, having spent a brief time in the company of the courageous Davis, I have seen at first-hand how vivid the memories of the situations faced by these unique characters remain.

It presses home the events all of the war weary had to live with, day in and day out, while carrying out their duty. To be able to push these to one side and return to normal life, so often picking up where they left off and slotting back into football as though they had never been away, is a true testament to the mental strength of what is a unique group of men.

It would be safe to assume that the grim realities of war must have helped to put sport in perspective for those who served in the forces. Maybe it even helped to give them a freedom to express themselves in a football arena that, after all, was far from the life and death environment they had found themselves embroiled in elsewhere.

Which brings us back to the beginning; as supporters, journalists, players and managers we are all guilty at times of taking football too seriously. It is treated very much as a 'life and death' pursuit, an intensity that has given the Scottish game the passion that has brought such glowing praise from far and wide.

Nobody would ever want to strip that away – but from time to time it pays to take a step back and reflect on what has gone before and consider the sacrifices made so readily by the players of the past.

Hero is a word that is perhaps over used in sport, but even the briefest delve into the history books proves that our game has been blessed with true heroes dating back almost a century to the start of the Great War. Theirs is a legacy worth preserving and a story worth retelling.

AN OFFICER AND A GENTLEMAN

The cemetery at Fauborg-d'Amiens is a world away from the industrial overtones of Rangers' heartland, but it is in the verdant and tranquil surroundings of the French graveyard, not in the red brick confines of Ibrox, that the story of the club's war heroes begins.

Inscribed on the Arras Memorial within the immaculately tended site are the names of 35,000 fallen soldiers from the British, South African and New Zealand forces who gave their lives between the spring of 1916 and summer of 1918 as the First World War death toll grew.

Among those engravings is the lasting tribute to the ultimate sacrifice made by Walter Tull; a hero, a gentleman and an individual who has risen posthumously to become an iconic figure capable of transcending the boundaries of football and war.

Books, documentaries, plays and monuments have all been created in Tull's memory. A memorial trophy and even a sports and arts trust have sprung up. The interest is intense and the affection limitless for a humble soldier who overcame prejudice with dignity and inspirational courage.

The character Tull displayed throughout his life in football and the forces was the embodiment of everything any team or regiment could look for in a team mate and comrade. Ready, willing and able.

He never pulled on the light blue jersey in competitive action or experienced the thrill of running out in front of a packed Ibrox Park – but Walter Tull has been adopted into the Rangers family. His dream was to serve his country and return to the sporting career in which he had starred, with the Englishman's heart set on completing a move to the Gers that had first been mooted before he set off to fight for his nation. Tull died with his light blue ambitions unfulfilled, but having pinned his colours to the mast he will never be forgotten on the south side of Glasgow. An honorary Bear.

The worldwide interest in the tale of Tull, his triumphs and tragedy, has demonstrated the depth of feeling that surrounds the Great War almost a century since the brutal conflict began. Time has passed and those fortunate enough to escape with their lives from the 1914 to 1918 battles have passed with it, but Britain will never forget.

Tull was among the nearly ten million military personnel who perished during those four bloody years. For decades it was left to those who survived the war to relay the true horror of the turmoil and pay testament to the heroics they witnessed. The death of Harry Patch in 2009, who at the grand old age of 111 was the last surviving British First World War veteran, closed the book on living history. Now only the vast records of the period remain as the lasting tribute to the millions who found themselves at the heart of the brave fight for freedom.

Those stories put modern day struggles in context and no-where more so than those centred around sportsmen of the era. While the millionaires of the twenty-first century football world are revered as heroes, their forebears from the early 1900s were the men who truly tested themselves in the face of adversity.

Walter Tull was just a month short of his thirtieth birthday when he died. Had he been parading his talents as a free-scoring forward in the modern day he would have been approaching that landmark celebration without a care in the world, save for concerning himself with how to spend the rich rewards showered upon players at the top of their game. Instead the reality for him and his peers was very different, with the weeks and months leading up to his thirtieth birthday dominated by the terrifying events which swept through the continent as the Great War drew to its conclusion.

Tull died on 25 March 1918, in frontline action. On 11 November the war ended, too late for the fallen soldiers who had made the ultimate sacrifice. He could not have known how close he had been to emerging from conflict and resuming normal civilian life and returning to action on the football field.

While Tull embraced army life, his first love had been sport and it was his prowess with a ball at his feet that had brought the Kent-born forward to the brink of a place on the Ibrox roll of honour. The son of a Caribbean carpenter who had landed on British shores in the second half of the nineteenth century, he entered the world in Felixstowe on 28 April 1888.

His English mother died just seven years later and his father also passed away while Tull was still a schoolboy, in 1897. At the age of nine he moved from the south coast to the inner city as he found a new home at the Bonner Road orphanage in Bethnal Green, at the heart of London's poverty-stricken East End. It was an incredibly tough start to life and the hard knocks continued to test Tull's resolve as his brother Edward, who had moved with him to London, was adopted by a Glaswegian family. It was this link to the west coast of Scotland that had tempted Tull to commit himself to a move Clydeside with Rangers years later, with his elder brother Edward Tull-Warnock established as a successful dentist in Glasgow, based at 419 St Vincent Street in the city centre.

While adoption had provided Edward with a route out of life as an orphan in London, it was football that gave his young brother a means of escape. Tull had first displayed his talents with the children's home team he represented and at the age of twenty he was recruited by Clapton FC. The dashing attacker helped his side to a string of amateur honours and after just a season was propelled into the professional game by Tottenham Hotspur, when he was signed in time for the 1909/10 campaign.

Spurs were preparing to take their place in the top flight for the first time and were scouring the London area for reinforcements to a squad which had won promotion from the Second Division at the first time of asking, narrowly missing out on the championship when Bolton Wanderers pipped them by a single point.

It brought Spurs a place in the First Division alongside capital rivals Arsenal and Chelsea at a time when England's north-south divide was prevalent. Newcastle United had reigned supreme in 1908/09 at the head of a northern charge for honours. Everton, Sunderland, Blackburn Rovers and Sheffield Wednesday made up the rest of the top five and set the pace for the southerners to aspire to.

Tull, having starred during a summer warm-up tour of South America, was quickly emerging as a key man as Spurs took their place at the top table. Reports of the time singled out the rising star as a player with intelligence and sparkling technique. Unfortunately supporters of rival teams singled him out for unwanted attention, with Tull's place as the first black player to play in England's elite league making him an easy target for racist abuse. One game, away to Bristol City in the autumn of 1909, is widely regarded as the turning point in Tull's fledgling career as a Tottenham player. The level of vitriol showered on the visiting Spurs man was noted in the press and the club's hierarchy reacted by dropping the victim to the reserves.

Whether it was to protect Tull or shield the team from unwanted attention, the result was that his assets were seldom utilised in the side from that point on. He played just a handful of additional first team games for Tottenham, who edged clear of relegation in what should have been a memorable first year as a senior player for Tull. Instead his team mates ploughed their furrow without the influential forward as they clawed their way out of the bottom two with a late season burst, which saw them climb to the sanctuary of fifteenth spot in the twenty-team league. It was city adversaries Chelsea and former promotion rivals Bolton Wanderers who fell through the trapdoor. Spurs went on to consolidate their place in the First Division the following year, but their efforts to establish themselves as a force to be reckoned with would continue without Tull.

While he had been pushed to the background at White Hart Lane, his ability had not been forgotten by those who had watched with interest as he burst onto the scene in his early days in a white shirt.

In 1911 it was Northampton Town who made the bold move. The fee was not disclosed, but the Cobblers were reported to have invested heavily to secure the services of a player who would in time become a club legend.

Northampton manager Herbert Chapman, who would become best known as one of Arsenal's most successful leaders, had unbending faith in his protégé. He installed Tull at the heart of his side, utilising him as a wing half as well as a forward. Indeed, in his first season with the club he scored nine goals in just a dozen matches including a four-goal haul against Bristol Rovers in his tally.

Town were at that stage featuring in the Southern League, not entering the main Football League structure until after the war. They were ambitious though, breaking a series of club transfer records as they built for the future.

In the three years between joining the East Midlands outfit and war breaking out Tull made more than 100 appearances on his way to becoming established as a fans' favourite among the appreciative Northampton faithful. Indeed, an eight-foot tall marble statue of the great man now stands proudly outside the Sixfields Stadium in the Garden of Rest, and the approach road has been named Walter Tull Way in honour of one of their most famous football sons.

While Tull honed his skills in the earthy surroundings of England's non-league grounds, Rangers were dominating the sport north of the border. League championships in 1911/12 and 1912/13 set William Wilton's team apart as the team of the moment and, with his family ties to Glasgow, there is no doubt Tull would have been well aware of the football landscape in Scotland. It was an environment he soon expressed a burning desire to experience at first-hand, although events in the wider world quickly overtook football concerns.

On 28 June 1914, the assassination of Austro-Hungarian monarch Archduke Franz Ferdinand in Bosnia-Herzegovina sparked the chain of events that led to the outbreak of the First World War. On 28 July the Austrians declared war on Serbia, having been assured of military support by their German neighbours, and Russia quickly mobilised in defence of the Serbs. France were next to instigate their involvement, siding with the Russia-Serbia alliance, and soon found themselves as a target for the German forces. When the Germans invaded French territory through Belgium there was a swift call to arms by British political leaders and the long war began.

On 21 December 1914, as tens of thousands of men across the United Kingdom prepared for frontline service, Tull led by example and became the first member of the Northampton Town playing staff to sign up with the army. He was enlisted in the Football Battalion's 17th Middlesex Regiment.

The general appeal for recruits had been targeted at men in the nineteen to thirty age group. Military chiefs quickly realised that sport represented a ripe ground for unearthing fit and determined characters, with the football unit used as a tool to encourage both professional and amateur players to join together with a new common purpose.

The British authorities enlisted prominent literary figures of the time to prepare propaganda material and rally existing and prospective troops. Scots writer Sir Arthur Conan Doyle joined that heavyweight cast and during a recruiting speech in September 1914 he directly targeted the nation's sportsmen. Conan Doyle said:

There was a time for all things in the world. There was a time for games, there was a time for business, there was a time for domestic life. There was a time for everything, but there is only time for one thing now, and that thing is war. If the cricketer had a straight eye let him look along the barrel of a rifle. If a footballer had strength of limb let him serve and march in the field of battle.

The address was designed to inspire players who, as a group, had been criticised in some quarters for not responding quickly enough to the cause. The verbal volleys came from high office, not least from the body of the church.

The Bishop of Chelmsford reflected growing public opinion when he spoke early in December 1914, with reports of the time noting:

The Bishop, in an address on Duty, spoke of the magnificent response that had been made to the call to duty from the King. All must play their part. They must not let their brothers go to the front and themselves remain indifferent. He felt that the cry against professional football at the present time was right. He could not understand men who had any feeling, any respect for their country, men in the prime of life, taking large salaries at a time like this for kicking a ball about. It seemed to him something incongruous and unworthy.

As if in direct response, just ten days later the 17th Service (Football) Battalion of the Middlesex Regiment was established on 12 December 1914. England and Bradford defender Frank Buckley is believed to have been the first professional to volunteer and, given his previous army experience, was awarded the rank of lieutenant before rising to become a major.

The Battalion attracted 600 men within months, with around 120 experienced football players bolstered by the addition of hundreds of additional individuals who had been tempted by the promise of serving alongside some of their sporting heroes. Entire professional teams signed up – including every member of the Clapton Orient squad, better known now as Leyton Orient.

Early in his training, as a dedicated Lance Sergeant, Tull was sent forward to Les Ciseaux. Stationed close to the French frontline, the rookie soldier was returned to home soil suffering from what is now known as post-traumatic stress disorder. The stark events in France had quickly become apparent.

It was in September 1916 that Tull was pressed back into action across the channel. The Battle of the Somme, which had claimed the life of England international Evelyn Lintott, was reaching a crashing climax as the final months of that notorious pocket of dogged fighting that cost the lives of hundreds of thousands of British soldiers was played out. Early in 1916 four members of the football unit had been killed and many more injured; in the autumn of that year the casualty count grew, with fourteen members killed by a poison gas attack launched by the Germans.

Over the course of four months on the battlefields of the Somme, Tull's exceptional ability as a soldier and his courage in the face of such heavy fighting won him the admiration of his comrades. He was promoted to become a sergeant and then nominated as an officer. In December Tull was posted back to Britain to train for that new role. A six-week period of leave allowed him to prepare for the challenges ahead and early in February 1917 he arrived at Gailes in Scotland to join the 10th Officer Cadet Battalion.

Army rules were clear; no soldier of 'non-European' descent was eligible for officer status. Tull, as he had done on the football field years earlier, broke the mould and flew in the face of convention. In May that year he was commissioned as an officer and, as a 2nd Lieutenant, became the first black man to command white troops in the British army.

The officer training programme was thorough but intense. More than four months were spent in the confines of Gailes, the sprawling training camp sandwiched on the west coast between Troon and Irvine. Hundreds of accommodation units sprung up around the complex, which was pressed into action during both the Great War and Second World War. As many as 600 men would muster in Ayrshire at one time to be pushed through the programme and learn the ropes under expert tutelage. A succession of Scottish regiments used Gailes, including the Cameronians and the Royal Scots Fusiliers. It was a hive of activity as those classed as leadership material were shipped in and pushed out, officers being hastily equipped to spearhead the next phase of the assault on the continent. Some moved to France while others ventured further afield and Tull was in the latter group as he received his orders after completing his training.

He established an exemplary record as an officer, travelling to the frontline in Italy and leading his men on two raids across the River Piave without loss of life. Just as the media had noted his unflappable approach on the sporting field, he was similarly mentioned in dispatches for his calm attitude under pressure on the battlefield. His gallantry was also remarked upon and led to a recommendation for the Military Cross, although that honour was never bestowed upon the remarkable Tull. A concerted campaign has since been mounted to have the medal awarded posthumously, which as yet has not borne fruit.

Leading the campaign to have Tull's bravery formally recognised is Northampton South MP Brian Binley, who passionately supports the assertion that the Military Cross would be a fitting commemoration of the officer's actions in battle.

The argument from the Home Office has always been that a posthumous award would set a precedent that would lead to an influx of new cases being put forward, and that the rules of the era, as discriminatory as they were, had to be obeyed.

There were strong signs that those in power were willing to bend when, in 2007, Maori soldier Haane Manahi, a Second World War soldier from New Zealand, was honoured in a ceremony attended by Prince Andrew. Binley said:

Walter Tull has become an important inspiration in today's multi-racial Britain and he has become a role model for many young people in our schools in Northampton, Bristol, Folkestone and many other areas of the country.

Walter was recommended for a medal and there is a strong suspicion that he didn't receive it because the rule of the day said that a man of colour couldn't be an officer in the field, and consequently the War Department might have been embarrassed by the attention created if Walter was rewarded for his just deserts. Not only did Walter Tull fight and die for his country but he clearly inspired so many people whilst he was alive and it is the quality of the man as well as his bravery which requires recognition.

After success in Italy, Tull and his men transferred to the Somme. It had been the scene of his earlier heroics, but this time the experience would have no such happy ending for the officer and gentleman.

On 25 March 1918, after days of facing a desperate onslaught from the advancing Germans, Tull was killed by machine-gun fire near the Favreuil airbase. His horrified charges in the 23rd (2nd Football Battalion) Middlesex Regiment made gallant efforts to retrieve the body of their respected leader. Leicester City goalkeeper Tom Billingham laid his own life on the line to mount a rescue attempt, but had to retreat. Tull's body was never recovered.

Rather than a burial plot, the memories are kept alive by his place on the Arras memorial and the other tributes that have been created closer to home. Deep in Scotland family photographs and mementoes of his career in the army and in football are retained with pride.

Tull's roots may lie in the Caribbean, Kent and London but he retains a very strong tartan connection through his surviving family north of the border. In a corner of the Highlands, his relatives still proudly remember their famous ancestor with warmth and affection.

It was Edward Tull-Warnock, as the footballer's brother became known following his adoption to his Glasgow family, who established the Scottish bloodline. Tull-Warnock, who like his more famous brother broke down barriers in a different field by becoming Britain's first black dentist, served patients in Glasgow, Girvan and Aberdeen. In Glasgow at the time his St Vincent Street surgery was at the heart of a thriving city centre, at the far end of the street now established as a residential beat.

His reach has since stretched further north through his daughter, Jean. It was Jean's marriage to Highland minister Reverend Duncan Finlayson that provides the lasting link between the Tull family and Scotland, with the Finlaysons settling in the village of Strathpeffer and settling down to have a family of their own. Their daughter, Pat Justad, still lives in the charming north spa village and owns the Green Kite Trading shop at the heart of the community.

Pat recounts her formative years being filled with stories of the achievements of her grandfather's lauded brother. Pictures of Walter Tull adorned the walls of the family home and tales of his daring on the football pitch and in army uniform gave her a sense of the great man's standing. For any youngster the play-ground bragging rights gained by having a famous footballer in the family were worth extra kudos – the Finlaysons of Strath-peffer had a war hero in the self same package.

Pat Justad told me:

It has always been an intriguing family to be part of. The other half are all Highlanders who can trace their roots right back to the Battle of Culloden – so it's an interesting mix to say the least. When you have grown up with it, you don't tend to think too much about the story. It is just part and parcel of the family history – but when you sit back and think about everything, there are some incredible aspects.

Walter was always a family hero, long before he became a public hero. It is really only in recent years that his life and achievements have been picked up by a wider audience. We were brought up knowing all about his achievements, with photographs on the wall, and have always been proud of him and my grandfather, Edward Tull-Warnock, who had to overcome prejudice in his own life. They both had to overcome incredible adversity.

The images that have become a familiar presence for Justad and her family are among the few surviving hints at her famous footballing relative's notable work in sport and in the army.

She explained:

We had Walter's football medals and his war medals in the family until the 1960s, when they were stolen. They have never been recovered. When Walter died his possessions passed to Edward, as his next of kin, and were subsequently passed on to my father. It was while Dad was working as a minister in Monifieth that the medals were stolen from a safe, along with the church silver.

The communion silver was found dumped in bushes not too far away, presumably because it would have been too difficult to sell on, but the medals have never been found. There have been attempts since then to try and track them down but there has been no joy. It would be wonderful to think that one day the medals would turn up and could be returned to the family.

Even though we no longer have those medals, we do have some mementoes that relate particularly to Walter's war experiences. There are letters, photographs and postcards that my granddad kept as well as a Deutschmark note taken from a captured German soldier.

Somewhere out there are the medals of a true British war and football hero. The hope for Tull's surviving family is that they have survived intact, although investigations at the time of the theft and subsequent efforts to trace the treasured pieces of family history have both drawn a blank.

Their grandfather, Edward Tull-Warnock, was a noted sportsman in his own right. While forging a successful career in dentistry he also established a reputation as a fine golfer on the amateur circuit in Scotland. The surviving relatives are understandably proud of their ancestry, with tales of the achievements of both Tull brothers never far from the minds of those who have continued the family name.

It is the Scottish section of the family which provides the strongest clue as to the validity of the claims that Walter Tull was either a signed Rangers player, or at the very least an Ibrox star in waiting, when he was killed in action. There is little doubt in their mind that the switch into light blue would have taken place had tragedy not struck, and the anecdotal evidence shows a long-standing link between the family and Rangers Football Club, a link that in the days long before football agents and players' unions was far more useful in securing future employment for a player seeking a fresh challenge than it is possible to imagine. It was word of mouth and the far-reaching Ibrox network in Glasgow that led to moves to put a Gers shirt on Tull's back gathering momentum, as club officials discovered his availability and willingness to settle north of the border.

Methodist minister Reverend Finlayson, whose wife Jean passed away in 2004, married into the Tull family and has been captivated by their illustrious past. He explained:

> Edward, my father-in-law, was a very fine footballer in his own right. He could have played for Rangers himself, I'm sure. Dad, as I always called Edward, turned out for Ayr Parkhouse in the days when the club was the equivalent of a senior team and also for Girvan at the same level.
>
> He always had a close connection with Girvan, so much so that when he went into practice in Glasgow he also established a practice in Girvan and bought a house in the town. He was already well known in the area through his football and for many years he was the only dentist in Girvan. When his sister Sissy moved up from England, to look after his adoptive mother after she had suffered a stroke, it was the house in Girvan that she lived in, so the family had strong links to that area.

The Ayr Parkhouse club that Tull-Warnock featured for has been consigned to the history books, but in the early part of the twentieth century the team was a major player in the Scottish game. Founded in 1886, Parkhouse became the town's third senior club three years later when they stepped up to join Ayr Football Club and Ayr Athletic. As Ayr struggled to support the trio of clubs, Athletic were disbanded soon after. Parkhouse maintained an amateur tradition but joined the nation's leading clubs in 1902 when they were admitted to the Scottish Football League's Second Division. After just a single season in that company, Parkhouse lost their place as Aberdeen stepped into the league set-up. In 1905 the club turned professional and went on to return to the SFL ranks in 1906, although it remained a rocky road. In 1910 Ayr FC and Ayr Parkhouse joined forces, after years of wrangling over a potential amalgamation, to form the Ayr United name that is more familiar to Scottish football supporters today.

It was amid the changing face of football on the west coast that Edward Tull-Warnock began to immerse himself in the Scottish game, and along the way he won many friends and admirers, some of whom would prove central to his brother's ambitions of playing north of the border.

Reverend Finlayson said:

Edward played football with James Bowie, who would later go on to become chairman of Rangers after first playing for the club. The two were very close friends. I don't know how that friendship began but I do know that when Dad moved into the west end of Glasgow there were a few neighbours who would not speak to him on the grounds of the colour of his skin. Through all of that adversity, he also struck up some wonderful friendships with those who did welcome him.

It could have been in those circumstances that he and Jimmy Bowie became close, it could have been football or it may even have stemmed from his time at Alan Glen's School. What we do know is that Jimmy Bowie and his wife were good family friends with the Tull-Warnocks.

My wife, Jean, attended many games at Ibrox with her father in the directors' box and grew quite bored of it – she would far rather have been at the pictures with her mother. Dad was of course in Girvan doing his dentistry on Saturdays, so there were only certain occasions when they could make it along to games. However, in later years if ever we needed tickets for international matches or big fixtures they were always made available through Jimmy.

That friendship would be significant in the link between Walter and Rangers. Jimmy Bowie would have been aware of Walter's standing as a professional footballer through Edward and I am sure that is where the interest would have come from.

Where the debate lies is in just how advanced the discussions between Walter Tull and Rangers had been prior to his death. The family know that Tull had already made his mind up to move to the west coast as, after years of living apart following their separation at the time of Edward's adoption and move to Scotland, the brothers planned for a future closer together.

Like so many soldiers in the Great War, Tull had dreams of completing his service and carving out a new life free of the horrors of battle. No doubt those visions helped carry him through the darkest times in the trenches, although for Tull there was to be no happy ending. The script he had plotted involved a family reunion in Glasgow and the exhilaration of running out at Ibrox. Enemy troops put paid to the best laid plans.

Reverend Finlayson said:

To be an officer was like a sentence of death at that time, particularly on the Somme where Walter ended up. The war was such a terrible waste of life, all because two Royal brothers had a quarrel.

Walter's intention was quite clear that when the war was over he was moving up to Glasgow. Edward was there and his sister Sissy was there by that point. It is clear from correspondence that he would come to Glasgow and even though he was in the eventide of his career as a footballer he was a player who interested Rangers.

The story that he had in fact gone as far as joining Rangers first came out in a newspaper in the 1940s, when he was described as having signed for the club. Whether that is true I cannot say, and that is also the case with the suggestion that he had played for Rangers as a guest. It is certainly my understanding that he had turned out for the club while he was going through officer training at Wester Gailes, but I don't have any hard and fast evidence of that.

The surviving family are understandably proud of both brothers, happy to keep alive the achievements of both men whenever possible. Indeed, in modern times there have been gentle reminders of Walter Tull's place in the Ibrox story.

Reverend Finlayson added:

I wrote to Rangers when Graeme Souness was in charge and signed Mark Walters. Much was made in the press of Walters being the first black outfield player to join Rangers, and in my letter I pointed out that in fact Walter Tull had been recruited many years before. The manager wrote back and thanked me for that information.

The arrival of Walters in the 1980s stoked up tensions in the Scottish game and brought the debate over racism among supporters to the fore. The furore created by his appearance in the Premier Division, and the response from followers of some rival teams, proved that, unfortunately, the nation still had a major problem to address.

For relatives of Tull, this was no surprise. Their ancestors had seen it before and come through it with a mixture of strength and faith.

Reverend Finlayson explained:

The Methodist church runs right through the Tull story. Edward was a great Methodist and when I went to him to ask for his lovely daughter's hand in marriage he said to me, 'Do you know what you are doing? Your children could be as black as me.' He told me some of his own stories, one in particular about the occasion when he qualified as the best student in Glasgow, and went for his first job as an assistant, as dentists had to do. He sent off an application for a job in Birmingham and dutifully enclosed a photograph. He got the job and travelled south, complete in the suit and watch and chain that his adoptive father had bought him for starting work. He arrived in Birmingham and knocked on the door – the man answered, took one look at Edward and said 'Good god, you're coloured – you'll destroy my practice overnight!' His next appointment was in Aberdeen, and while he was in the north-east he went to the Methodist church in the city, where he met the senior Baillie of Aberdeen and then his daughter, who in time became his wife. If not God himself then the Methodist church moves in mysterious ways.

Edward Tull-Warnock and Walter Tull overcame racism in England and Scotland in all spheres of their lives; from football, the army and professional circles through to everyday living. In the face of those challenges they excelled in every pursuit and have become important social figures for so many reasons.

While for the Scots in the Tull clan the name is a glance back to their family's past, the name has become something far different yet equally valuable in the south of England. There the Tull tag has become a beacon for diversity groups, with a number of organisations fostering the story of adversity, triumph and tragedy to fit in with their own aims and message. He has been held up as an inspiration and a motivation for a new generation of sports fans who can still relate to the challenges faced by a player who lived in a football environment that, aside from the nuts and bolts of the game, bears little semblance of similarity to the modern game.

In 2006, the Walter Tull Sport, Music and Arts Development Association was founded in Bristol. The group works under the banner of being an organisation 'Run by human beings for the betterment of human beings, whoever they are and wherever they come from'. You have to imagine the man who lends his name to this charity would have nodded his approval to that key objective. The hope is to continue to develop the concept of black and Asian mentors, almost a century after the death of the character who could be held up as the finest ambassador for diversity in both sport and the armed forces. The Tull Association's work quickly earned plaudits, not to mention tens of thousands of pounds of lottery funding, and won the group representation at Downing Street, a far cry from its hero's humble beginnings as the son of an immigrant.

Youth worker Beresford Lee is the man who came up with the concept for the association and he worked hard to put it on the map, as if somehow making up for the racial gauntlet run by Tull all those years ago when he was subjected to a torrent abuse in front of the Bristol City supporters. After the formation of the association, a team of mentors was pulled together to go out into schools in the South West of England and tell the incredible story of Tull to a young, impressionable and receptive audience.

Speaking after the project passed its four-year milestone, Lee said:

I wanted to find a way to engage with school children about the subject of racism and I also wanted to find a role model for young people to look up to. All too often they look up to modern-day stars who might not always be the best role models. I realised from what I'd read about Walter Tull, he would make an excellent role model.

He was a man who pulled himself up out of poverty; he was brought up in a London orphanage. He was spotted by a football scout while playing in the street with his friends. Then he went on to become one of the big footballing stars of his day, despite the sort of prejudice against black players that manifested itself so terribly here in Bristol.

While football continues to be dogged by incidents of prejudice, the modern environment is far removed from those early days of the game. The brave pioneers like Tull helped to pave the way towards a more tolerant approach, even if there is still work to be done.

Lee added:

It's good to know that we have come such a long way as a society. We may still get occasional racist outbursts from football crowds but these days, when it does happen, it's coming from a tiny minority who are only interested in extolling their extremist views. The terrible thing about Walter's case was that the abuse he experienced was very common back then. Casual racism was the norm at the time. Even the match reports referred to Walter as 'Darkie' Tull.

On every front and in every chapter of his life, Tull had to overcome the type of adversity that simply cannot be imagined in modern-day Britain. On each occasion he found an obstacle in his path, Tull negotiated past it and continued stronger. In the end only the bullets of the enemy could bring him down.

From his start in life as a young orphan to the horrifying prejudice that threatened his football career, the incredible story of Walter Tull featured the discrimination he so gallantly overcame to rise to become a heroic officer in the British Army and then the horrors of life, and death, at war. He was months away from a new life as a football star with Rangers, living side by side with his beloved brother in what was destined to become the family's adopted home in Glasgow. Instead he made the ultimate sacrifice for his country.

Tull's tale is a tragic story punctuated by inspirational acts and examples of the type of dogged attitude that pervaded throughout times of war. The honorary Ranger led the way but was not alone in his bravery and spirit, as the stories of the many men who shared a Rangers jersey with a services uniform, through not only the First World War and Second World War but a host of conflicts across globe, can attest.

2

SILVERWARE AND SACRIFICES

The campaign to have Walter Tull formally recognised for his bravery in the field is gallantly marching on. Whether the effort bears fruit remains to be seen, but for a long line of men with Rangers connections the honours of the Great War were bestowed with no such delay.

Medals were presented as the courage of the Scots among the proud British fighting force came to the fore in the harshest surroundings and among the celebrated number was a certain Finlay Balantyne Speedie.

The Dumbarton boy became an Ibrox legend during the early years of the twentieth century as he helped his club establish itself as a major force in the fledgling Scottish league system.

By the time the First World War broke out, Speedie was well into his thirties and in the twilight of his playing career. The light blue of Rangers had been swapped for the colours of his hometown team Dumbarton by that stage and when he departed Scottish shores for service on the continent it marked a formal conclusion to the end of his days on the park. Although Speedie returned from the Great War alive, albeit wounded in action, there was no playing comeback. Instead he focused on passing on his huge experience as a coach.

His reputation as a fine player at the highest level held him in good stead as he embarked on the period of his life in the post-war years – but in addition, his achievements in the army would also have enhanced the huge respect in which he was held in the aftermath of a conflict that touched so many families directly.

Speedie found himself among the first wave of recipients of the Military Medal, one of a number of Rangers men to have been honoured by their country with that particular award.

The medal was instituted in March 1916 and was designed to recognise what military leaders described as 'Acts of gallantry and devotion to duty performed by non-commissioned officers and men of our army in the field.' It sat side by side with the Military Cross, which was reserved for warrant and junior officers who had displayed similar courage in the field.

The silver circular design – fittingly coming complete with red, white and blue ribbon – was embossed with the head of King George V when it was introduced and as British troops poured onto the continent to fight the deserving cases quickly amassed. A recommendation from a commanding officer in the field was required for troops to be honoured, and Speedie gained that nomination in 1918 after a particularly torrid period of fighting on the Western Front.

Examples of acts that merited nomination included soldiers digging wounded or killed comrades from wrecked trenches after being bombarded by enemy mortar fire, battling on in the face of terrible injuries that would have grounded most others, venturing forward into enemy dugouts without thought for their own safety, carrying injured colleagues across treacherous battlefields to safety, or other similar endeavours well above and beyond the call of duty. Close and brutal contact with the enemy was common and day after day, hour after hour, troops faced life-and-death split-second decisions. They witnessed horrific events and tackled the grim assignments with fortitude and courage. A sense of duty was the motivation, not silverware, but for those singled out there was at least official confirmation of the appreciation of their superiors as well as a tangible reminder of the sacrifice they made while wearing the uniform of their nation.

Each honour was announced in the *London Gazette*, along with confirmation of each officer's commissions, and Speedie's entry was listed in August 1918. He was just two years short of his fortieth birthday when he had his gallantry commended, well above the average age of a combat soldier. With no strenuous vetting of age for conscripts, the army relied on the enthusiasm of a youthful contingent to bolster numbers. Speedie and the other older heads added the benefit of experience and proved that age was no barrier to bravery. The stamina, fitness and strength of character developed during his years as a professional sportsman transferred to his new role.

Individual citations were not printed in the *Gazette*, ensuring most have been lost to the mists of time. Recipients received a copy of their citation at the time, although understandably very few are readily accessible since they were swallowed up in private possessions rather than formal archives. While some details can be found in histories of individual units or in local newspaper archives, the majority of medal holders are recorded only by name rather than by deed.

Speedie's bravery in the field made him one of more than 115,000 servicemen to be rewarded for their heroics in the First World War. Around two per cent of all those had their achievements and honours listed publicly for all to see. The process was a relatively simple one, with battlefield commanders able to send their recommendations back to headquarters for consideration by the higher powers in the forces. These suggestions were rubber-stamped and the honour subsequently formally announced via the *London Gazette* and notification sent to the recipient.

Foreign soldiers and, unusually for the time, women were also eligible for the Military Medal, with French and Americans among the recipients. For Brits, the individual's name and regiment was engraved around the edge of the medal and many of the historic pieces of sentimentally precious metal circulate on the comprehensive collectors' market today. Those issued to servicemen from overseas carried no name.

The equivalent awards for those in the other forces at the time were the Distinguished Service Medal for exemplary gallantry at sea and the Distinguished Flying Medal for exemplary gallantry in the air.

Carefully crafted copies of various medals have also sprung up, usually denoted as such when advertised, as the unquenchable thirst for military memorabilia from the Great War shows no sign of abating.

Although the Military Medal is the most common of the First World War awards, the appreciation of the recipients has not been diluted. Museums the length and breadth of Britain display the medals proudly and have welcomed donations from some of the most unlikely of sources. Whether presented by family members or unearthed during allotment digs, thousands of the medals have been preserved for the best part of a century.

The flow of awards slowed after the First World War, with less than 16,000 medals issued, but the medal continued to be bestowed in limited numbers for decades after. Less than 1,000 were distributed throughout the 1950s, '60s, '70s and '80s. It was not until 1993 that the Military Medal was discontinued, with the Ministry of Defence ruling that the Military Cross should be made available to all ranks from that point on in cases of bravery in the presence of the enemy.

The whereabouts of Finlay Speedie's Military Medal is unknown, but what is certain is that its association with a man held so dearly in the history of the Rangers Football Club makes it all the more valuable. The daring deeds of that honest generation of sporting stars are well regarded by modern collectors.

Over the course of more than half a century, Midlands-based auction house Warwick and Warwick has established a wealth of experience in the field. Recognised as one of the leading auctioneers of collectables in Britain, the company has a dedicated military medal specialist to value and pull together the collections which fall under the hammer in specialist sales six times a year. Medals from early and Victorian campaigns to the Boer War and both World Wars prove popular, with many others passing through the Warwick auction house to a keen and appreciative audience every second month. The popularity of the military sales continues to grow.

Paul Murray is the man charged with leading the department and his passion for the subject stems from his own collection. Murray told me:

> I got into the job because I was a collector. It was very much a hobby which turned into something more and I am very fortunate to be able to work in an area that holds such great appeal to me. I get to deal with many fascinating collections and individual pieces on a daily basis. My own particular interest is in medals from the Zulu War and World War One and my collection reflects that.

So, just how do football and war come together in the intriguing and competitive world of militaria? The answer is simple. Just as the thirst for football sells newspapers, sells books and sells satellite television subscriptions it also transfers into the more niche surroundings of the auction house. Medals belonging to footballers have fallen under the hammer previously and the trend has been for a notable spike in both interest and value attributed to the buzz created by the appearance on the scene of an honour with a back story that has an extra dimension to it.

Murray said:

> While my own collection doesn't contain any medals that belonged to footballers, I am well aware there is a lot of interest in the military honours of sportsmen. The more interesting the player, the more valuable a medal is likely to become. Anyone connected to a club as big as Rangers would obviously be of great interest, not just to supporters of the team but to collectors in general. The challenge for every collector is in discovering more about the recipient of a particular medal and the story of the recipient is very important when it comes to making an accurate valuation.

While an established and authentic pedigree adds noughts to the value of any given lot, for the enthusiasts the challenge is unearthing a gem with a hidden past and putting flesh on the bones of the briefest of details. A name engraved upon a medal can lead to a trail that takes a new owner on a journey back in time that eventually brings a colourful story to life and adds to the significance of their latest collection piece. Finding a medal with a link to a sportsman with the type of heritage Speedie boasts is a eureka moment for any military aficionado with a sporting bent.

Warwick and Warwick's most recent experience of military medals with a sporting twist related to golf, not football. In December 2010 the First World War service medals of Abe Mitchell passed through the auction house and created quite a stir on the back of their famous recipient.

The Englishman was a notable player, coming to the fore in the years after serving with the Royal Artillery in France during the war. He had been capped by England as an amateur prior to seeing action of a different kind under the British flag and then, as a professional, won a number of tournaments and was a contender for the Open championship several times in the 1920s.

Mitchell spent three years in America serving as coach to Samuel Ryder, the man who put his name to the Ryder Cup. Mr Ryder did not, however, put his face to the famous trophy – instead he chose the figure of Abe Mitchell to adorn the top of the cup in recognition of Mitchell's efforts in tutoring him. Mitchell went on to play in the Ryder Cup three times and was regarded as one of the finest players never to win a Major.

Mitchell's standing in the game of golf ensured a premium was placed on his service medals when they came to be sold, bolstered by the existence of documentation charting Mitchell's exploits with club in hand. The collection in itself was not spectacular but the famous recipient ensured a higher than average estimate of £400. The imagination of the buying public was, not surprisingly, captured and in the end the hammer fell with the price at £977, hugely outstripping expectations and causing a real buzz in the sale room. It was an indication of just how much a sporting provenance can add to the value of otherwise standard militaria.

Service medals are naturally more commonplace and, in general terms, less valuable than gallantry medals. For example, a First World War Western Front Military Cross and Distinguished Conduct Medal group sold in February 2011 for close to £3,000 without the added attraction of any sporting heritage.

Murray said:

As you move up the scale, the price increases. A Military Medal should fetch between £300 and £700 depending what else they come with, while a Military Cross would range from £800 to

£1,500 when factors such as the regiment and the details of the citation are taken into account. No two medals are the same and the strength of the citation can be very important. The detail of the acts that had earned the recipient the honour were published for all Military Cross awards but not for the Military Medal, due to the large quantities that started to be issued. Instead only brief details were published. Some can be found in the war diaries kept by the battalions but they can be difficult to trace.

But who are the modern army who are perpetuating the interest in relics from a bygone era? According to a man who actively participates on both sides of the fence, as buyer and auctioneer, there is no stereotypical collector. Instead there is interest from a vast range of people who have struck up an interest in the honours passed to the brave individuals who fought for their country with distinction. Keen amateurs mingle with dealers and ardent collectors, some purchasing for their own entertainment and others choosing to display their finds and showcase the fruits of their research labour.

Murray said:

There is a wide spectrum of interest in military medals and it is very much a boom market. Some of the areas we deal with on a regular basis could be classed as having an ageing audience – for example stamp collections and cigarette cards. There is little interest in these from younger collectors but the opposite is true with the military medals, where I would say buyers range from aged in their twenties up. I go to medal fairs all over the country and it certainly isn't a case of them only attracting seventy-year-old blokes with experience or memories of war times.

What we find is that many younger collectors have developed an interest through either their fathers or grandfathers. However, more and more the interest stems from the growing interest in ancestry. That growth in research has undoubtedly had a positive influence on the market for medals and we find some people will collect to a certain family name, particularly if it is an uncommon one.

As an established member of the Smith clan, perhaps I will abandon my career as a militaria collector before it has even begun. However, for many others the attraction is strong and the appeal is heightened by the fact that you do not have to be a millionaire to participate. Just like art and antiques, the burgeoning medal market is very much a broad church that is open to all. Naturally it stands to reason that the deeper the pockets the more remarkable the artefacts available – but even if the budget is limited there are bargains to be had.

Murray said:

A collection can be started for a relatively modest sum. The most basic of First World War service medals, which were awarded to anyone who saw service overseas and included the British War Medal and Victory Medal, can be bought for as little as £25 or £30. A lot depends on the regiment, with those attached to the service corps less sought after because they were bigger and saw less action than the artillery.

Ironically, the boom in interest in the ageing military items can be traced to the advent of internet technology. Now, with information at the fingertips of every budding collector, there is a more informed audience to play to for the auctioneers. No longer are dusty tomes in hushed libraries the only source of background and for armchair ancestry sleuths the world is very much their oyster. That makes medal shopping all the more entertaining and very often buyers are arriving armed with every last cough and spit of background relating to recipients of particular honours appearing in sales catalogues up and down the country.

Murray added:

So much depends on the background to each medal or collection and the sphere has changed beyond all recognition in recent years. Previously, research was nigh on impossible unless you were prepared to spend time at the national archive in London. Now, with the advent of online ancestry sites and more and digital archives that are more widely accessible from home, it is possible to learn more about the recipient.

The stream of medals coming onto the market shows no sign of drying up. With hundreds of thousands of honours awarded during the peak war years, it is unlikely demand will ever outstrip supply. While many medals remain firmly entrenched in the families of the recipients, others are finding their way onto the open market through a variety of avenues. For dedicated collectors there is no sadness that medals are breaking free from the shackles of hereditary handovers, with the theory going that by breaking the family chain there is an opportunity to breathe new life into the honours and bring the stories of the recipients back to life.

Murray explained:

We see medals coming out of families quite regularly now. If you do not have an interest now, it is unlikely that there will be in the future – so many people take the decision to release them to collectors who do have that interest. It is very understandable since, particularly with the First World War medals, very few surviving family members have any physical link with the recipients. They may not ever have met the relative who won the honour or remember them at all, so there is not that strong bond.

What happens next is quite often a revelation even for those who once had the medals in their possession. Armed with the silverware, medal collectors can use their considerable knowledge and expertise to piece together every last part of the military history of the recipient and quite often earn praise from the previous owners in the process. There should be no sadness about the process, according to Murray, since these treasures of an otherwise bleak period in British history deserve to be cherished and utilised to the full in an attempt to keep the sacrifices of that era fresh in the minds of a new generation.

Quite often auction lots that have lain hidden for decades are brought shining into the light to be given pride of place in museums up and down the land, loaned by proud new owners after being lovingly brought back to former glory with care and expertise. Every now and then a find that is out of the ordinary crops up and creates a stir among the medal fraternity, but there is passion for every medal that burns strong and keeps the hammer falling week in and week out. After all, there is no such thing as an 'ordinary' war hero.

Murray said:

A medal or collection that has sat gathering dust in a drawer for thirty years can be brought to auction and picked up by an enthusiast who will then do the research, find out the story behind the recipient and display the medal and information. It keeps the memory of these servicemen alive and many families feel pleased that by passing on the medals they are able to be part of that process.

The fact that Finlay Speedie had pulled on a Rangers jersey has helped to keep his achievements in the forces alive. He served as a private in the 8th Battalion of the Argyll and Sutherland Highlanders. Born on 18 August 1880, Speedie was a veteran footballer well into his thirties by the time he joined up to serve in the war and a relatively old head as part of a force that had attracted so many young men.

Fittingly when he set off on the path from sport to the services, he joined a regiment that had its own slice of football history. Plymouth Argyle may be far removed geographically from the proudly Scottish fighting force, but they owe their name, or at least half of it, to their friends from the north. The two enthusiasts who formed the south coast club are reported to have been impressed by the style with which the Argyll and Sutherland Highlanders' football team won the Army Cup while stationed in the Devon city in the latter part of the 1800s and adopted the moniker for their own new club. The green of Plymouth Argyle also matches the green of the Argyll tartan and the matching hackle sported by soldiers in the regiment.

When Speedie served in the Great War, he did so as part of a relatively new regiment. The Argyll and Sutherland Highlanders were an amalgamation of the 91st Princess Louise's Argyllshire and the 93rd Sutherland Highlanders. Military reform in 1881 brought the two together under one new banner with a common purpose. The regiment remained active until 2006 when the controversial decision to create a single Royal Regiment of Scotland was enforced. The proud name of the Argyll and Sutherland Highlanders may have been lost in terms of active service, but its achievements of the past will never be forgotten.

At the outset of the Great War the regiment was divided into four regular battalions, two militia battalions, seven service battalions and five territorial battalions. It was as part of one of those territorial groups that Speedie fought, with the volunteer 8th Battalion. That was one of ten from the Argyll and Sutherland Highlanders which were sent into battle in France and Flanders and tasked with the daunting role of joining the cause on the Western Front. A further four battalions were sent to the Mediterranean to join the effort there as the Scottish influence stretched into all corners of a war that had quickly enveloped large swathes of the continent.

Acts of incredible bravery were familiar to the regiment – with six Victoria Cross awards during the First World War for Argyll and Sutherland Highlanders' soldiers. The Victoria Cross winners, ranging between the summer of 1915 and the autumn of 1918, were Captain J.A. Liddell for his exploits in Belgium, Lieutenant J.R.N. Graham after service in Mesopotamia and the quartet of 2nd Lieutenant A. Henderson, 2nd Lieutenant J.C. Buchan, Lieutenant D.L. MacIntyre and Lieutenant W.D. Bissett for their heroics in France.

While the deeds of that select half dozen brought glowing praise, the less appealing statistics point to the loss of 6,906 officers and men during the course of the conflict. As the regiment's own historians point out, that number equates to the modern equivalent of the entire population of the region's main hub at Oban. It was a quite incredible loss of life on a scale that could not have been envisaged when the troops set off from their various bases early in the war.

So many of those men lost their lives in the opening months of the conflict, but Speedie was one of the number who were there through to the final throes. We know from his Military Medal award in the summer of 1918 that he stood and fought in the most crucial periods of the Great War and clearly did so with distinction.

During the spring of 1918 the British forces had come close to defeat. With the war in its fourth year, manpower was dwindling and the Allies found themselves stretched to breaking point. The situation brought major political ructions back in London, where the politicians cosseted at Westminster were a world away from the horrific conditions on the front.

In November 1917 the War Office told its commander in chief, Air Marshal Sir Douglas Haig, that replacing losses in the forces would not be possible. It was estimated by the government at the time that within a year the British would be more than 250,000 troops below strength. Haig, it is believed, thought a more realistic calculation would be a shortfall in excess of 450,000 men.

The shortage could be attributed to the decision to balance the needs of the forces with the reliance on manpower to keep the country's industrial heart beating. Men were required in ship-building as well as food production and forestry.

With numbers dwindling, demands on the remaining troops were increasing as the fronts defended by British men were extended at around the same time. It led to conflict between Haig and the Cabinet committee, particularly since the Germans were able to deploy additional men to the Western Front after a collapse in the east. When the understrength 5th Army of the Allies was all but destroyed on 18 March on the Somme, forced back some forty miles, it could have marked the beginning of the end.

Instead, reinforcements were sent forward as, between March and August 1918, an additional 544,000 troops were sent to France and a further 100,000 were redeployed from Italy and other outposts.

Finlay Speedie's battalion was part of the 15th (Scottish) Division and was heavily involved in some of the fiercest fighting for the duration of the war. In the final year, in which Speedie received his Military Medal, the troops came through the First Battles of the Somme, which built up through the spring of 1918 and took the men of the Argyll and Sutherland Highlanders into the First Battle of Bapaume and the First Battle of Arras.

By the summer they were engaged in the Battles of the Marne

– notably the Battle of Tardenois when the 15th (Scottish) Division were part of the group which took Buzancy during a concerted operation on the afternoon of 28 July. It was described in battle diaries as the 'most gruelling' day the division had yet encountered.

In the two days previously Finlay's division had taken on more than half a mile of the front from French troops, taking its total to a two-mile stretch opposite Buzancy. The village, complete with chateau, covered a quarter of a square mile and sat on the slope of a rolling hill above the Allied frontline.

The artillery of the 15th (Scottish) Division was vital to the battle plan, firing a barrage of shells and machine-gun fire as well as smoke to screen the stage for the combat. French forces provided flame throwers while an air patrol was also engaged.

The chateau was quickly taken but the village was more difficult to claim, with every house having to be cleared of enemy soldiers one by one. More than 100 men were captured but the Germans sent heavy reinforcements towards the village and, with the French back-up failing to materialise, pushed the British men out of Buzancy and back to their starting position. It was a bitter blow after such good initial progress.

As the rain fell and conditions deteriorated, there were to be other gains in the area for the Allies and the action dovetailed with the Battles of Soissonais and of the Ourcq, during which substantial ground was made up.

Within four months the perilous situation of the Allied forces had been turned around and victory was complete. Every regiment had played its part, not least those pressed into combat on the Western Front.

One of the most prominent memorials of the Somme battle-fields was built in honour of Speedie's regiment. The tall Celtic cross, towering above the landscape, was unveiled by the

Duke of Argyll in 1923, adjacent to Sunken Lane. A simple yet poignant Gaelic inscription on the memorial states: 'Friends are good on the day of the battle.'

For a man raised amid the camaraderie of the Ibrox dressing room, it was a sentiment that Speedie was no stranger to. While no parallels can be drawn between the experiences of the Great War and the sporting career that had gone before it, there is no question that the courage displayed by Finlay Speedie the solider would have surprised none of the Rangers supporters who had watched Finlay Speedie the footballer in action.

He had been plucked from the fertile breeding ground of junior football during the 1900/01 season. The forward had been plying his trade with Clydebank Juniors before getting his big break with Rangers and his determination shone through as he grasped the opportunity with both hands and set about making the most of the chance afforded to him by manager William Wilton.

When Speedie made his debut in Gers colours on 20 October 1900, in a home league fixture against struggling Dundee, he entered a team that was chasing a third consecutive championship.

Dumbarton, the club he had first sampled the professional game with, and Celtic had both won the First Division prize back to back in previous years but no club had succeeded in completing a hat-trick. Two defeats and a draw inside the first nine matches of the season had left the hopes in the balance for Wilton's men. Whether by chance, coincidence or design there was an incredible run following the introduction of the new recruit.

Speedie's first game, a 4-2 win against the Dens Park outfit, was the first of eleven straight victories on a march to the title flag. In those games Rangers, with the new-look forward line gelling instantly, rattled in a staggering forty-two goals.

The junior turned senior bagged five of them himself, most notably in the 2-1 Old Firm triumph at Ibrox on 1 January 1901. That vital result put the Light Blues six points clear of league rivals Celtic with three games to play and ensured the celebrations could begin in earnest. Speedie was more than eight months short of his twenty-first birthday when he netted against Celtic but already looked like an assured presence in the Number 10 shirt, linking perfectly at inside left with erstwhile flanker Alex Smith.

It was a golden era for Rangers and the forward line of Campbell, McPherson, Hamilton, Speedie and Smith was feared by rival supporters as much as it was revered by the Ibrox loyal who had been treated to the goal rush created by that combination of attacking talent. Of course, crowds were not as they have come to be accepted as norm at the modern-day Ibrox. In that first term of the new century the regular home fixtures attracted gates in the region of 10,000 and peaked at 30,000 for the Old Firm encounters.

The prolific Hamilton understandably gained star billing but the supporting cast was just as valuable to the team effort that brought glittering rewards. The promptings of Speedie from the left channel breathed life into Wilton's side and he remained a key man for years to come. The only disappointment for the young forward in his maiden campaign was the pain of the 1-0 defeat against Celtic in the Scottish Cup final – but his time would come.

First, in the 1901/02 campaign, was the more pressing business of four-in-a-row. Rangers edged past their rivals from the east end to claim the First Division once again and Speedie was at the centre of it all, missing just two games and second only to his sidekick Smith on the appearance list.

The 1902/03 season brought a reversal in fortunes for Rangers as their league domination drew to a close and the prized trophy was passed on to Hibernian, who had become champions of Scotland for the first time in the club's history.

By way of consolation, the Scottish Cup was returned to the Rangers trophy cabinet for the first time since 1898. There were seven ever-presents in the 1902/03 run and Speedie was among them, setting the ball rolling with a hat-trick in the first round tie against Auchterarder, as the Perthshire side were brushed aside 7-0. He kept his place in the side right the way through to the final against Hearts, playing in the original showdown at Celtic Park and the two subsequent replays as 1-1 and 0-0 draws were followed by a 2-0 victory.

By the time Speedie and his team mates lined up in the following season's Scottish Cup final against Celtic the show-piece game had taken residence at Hampden Park and a crowd of close to 65,000 turned out for the city derby. Speedie's double that day was not enough to prevent his side from falling to a 3-2 defeat and there was further disappointment in the league as Wilton's side dropped to fourth in the table.

Disappointment turned to crushing agony in 1904/05 as both the league and cup were snatched from within Rangers' grasp in the cruellest of fashions. First came a 3-1 reverse at the hands of Third Lanark in the Scottish Cup final replay and then, three weeks later, came a championship play-off match against Celtic after the two clubs had tied on forty-one points at the top of the First Division table. All roads led once more to Hampden, and again the journey back to the south side of the city was not a happy one as the team in green and white claimed the premier domestic prize in the tensest of circumstances.

For Speedie it had been a year of highs and lows. While the team had ended the campaign empty-handed, in black and white terms it had been his most profitable as a Rangers forward. Having hit double figures for the first time with the club in the 1903/04 season, with a dozen-goal haul across league and cup, he notched eighteen in 1904/05 and came within a goal of matching Hamilton's tally at the top of the goal-scoring chart.

Appearances were restricted in the season following and early in 1906/07 he was recruited by Newcastle United. The Scotsman was an instant hit, helping the club to become England's champions and winning hero status as part of that conquering Magpies team.

By then he was a fully-fledged Scotland international, having won a trio of caps while a Rangers player in 1903. Speedie made his debut in dark blue against Wales at Ninian Park in Cardiff and marked the occasion in style as he knocked home the only goal of the game. He followed that up with Scotland's first in a 2-1 win against England at Bramall Lane in Sheffield, as the plucky visitors fought back from a goal down to defeat the Auld Enemy on their own turf. Sandwiched between those two fine wins was a 2-0 reverse at the hands of Northern Ireland at Celtic Park.

Speedie went on to play for Oldham Athletic and Bradford City for brief periods before returning home to Dumbarton in 1909, helping the Sons to claim the Second Division title two years later and retiring from playing commitments in 1914. He revived his links with the Boghead club in the 1930s when he served on the coaching staff. Speedie died in February 1953 at the age of seventy-two, remembered as a decorated football star and war hero.

3

FOLLOWING THE FOOTSTEPS
OF LEGENDS

On 17 March 1906, a significant event took place in Glasgow. The match in question was, in relative terms, not important. Rangers, on their way to a fourth-place finish in the First Division, drew 1-1 with their cross-city hosts Partick Thistle, who would end the campaign just one place below the Light Blues. The attendance of around 8,000 Glaswegians was run of the mill. The weather was unremarkable. What was notable was the team fielded by William Wilton that afternoon and, in particular, the forward line.

For the first time the combination of James Speirs at inside forward and Finlay Speedie, on the right wing, lined up at Number 8 and Number 7 on the team sheet. The two men would play in two further matches together for Rangers at the tail end of the 1905/06 term and the beginning of the following campaign, before the latter moved on. What neither could have predicted at the time is that both would share another common bond as recipients of the Military Medal during the Great War.

While Speedie returned to civilian life on the west coast after his distinguished service, there was no such happy ending for Speirs. After being recognised for his bravery in July 1917, the

41

former Rangers star died in action just a month later. He was a year past his thirtieth birthday, cut down in his prime after surviving three years of service.

It was a tragic end to a remarkable life story that had brought such credit to the family name. James Hamilton Speirs was a Glaswegian born and bred. He was brought into the world in Govanhill, one of six children, and was part of a mining family. Both his father and grandfather had served in the pits but Speirs took a different direction when he left school at fifteen and found work as a clerk.

At the same time he, like so many of his peers, was enjoying a traditional football education in the hotbed of the junior game in his home city. After progressing through the juvenile ranks with his local team Annandale, it was with juniors Maryhill that he cut his teeth and, while still in his teens, was spotted by Rangers and joined the Ibrox cause. He had played just a smattering of games for Maryhill before earning promotion to the big stage in the summer of 1905.

The blue half of the city was still smarting after the indignation of being narrowly pipped to the league crown by Celtic in a championship play-off match at the end of the 1904/05 season.

He was a versatile forward, comfortable playing in any of the positions across the frontline, and quickly established himself in the first team. He made his debut against Port Glasgow in an away match in October 1905 and marked the occasion by scoring the fourth in a 4-1 victory against the perennial strugglers. The new recruit continued to find the net at regular intervals during the course of his maiden season, scoring half a dozen league goals in eighteen appearances and banging in a hat-trick in the Scottish Cup first round tie against Arthurlie as his side triumphed 7-1.

The club ended the year empty-handed and it was the same story in 1906/07, a period in which Speirs struck up a potent partnership with strike partner Archie Kyle. Both men were tied on thirteen goals each over the league campaign, with Speirs' goal against Galston in the Scottish Cup giving him the edge when the final totals were totted up. Speirs emerged from the season at the head of the club's scoring chart with a highly respectable haul of fourteen goals from just twenty-five appearances in both competitions.

The emergence of Robert Campbell in subsequent years began to marginalise Speirs at Rangers, although he continued to be a reliable performer when called upon. So much so that Scotland's selectors picked up on his talents in the spring of 1908, at a time when the forward was struggling to hold down a club place.

He swapped light blue for dark blue on 7 March 1908, when he took his place in the famous Scotland Number 9 shirt to line up against Wales in the home international championship. The match was taken out of Glasgow and played in the more compact surroundings of Dens Park in Dundee, with the hosts bouncing back from a 1-0 deficit at half-time to win 2-1 with goals after the break from Alec Bennett and Aberdeen's William Lennie. It proved to be a first and last taste of the international game for Speirs, although it transpired the Rangers man's finest football hour was yet to come.

His Ibrox time drew to a close in 1908 and he left the ground empty-handed, having served during a rare barren spell for the club. After a brief stop with Clyde, his sporting journey took him south and away from the comfort of Glasgow and its surroundings – but Speirs flourished in his new environment.

The resilient Scot found a new home with Bradford City and became a legend with the Bantams as he was installed as captain with the English top flight side, and led them to glory in the FA Cup in 1911. It was a remarkable season for the Yorkshiremen, who climbed to fifth in the league to record what remains their highest ever placing. Of course the cup run was the most celebrated aspect of a memorable year. New Brompton, Norwich City, Grimsby Town, Burnley and Blackburn Rovers were all accounted for before the final showdown with Newcastle United. The first match, at Crystal Palace, ended in a goalless stalemate but the Old Trafford replay turned in Bradford's favour when the influential Speirs headed home the only goal of the match to land the coveted trophy for his club after an end-to-end match. Speirs led his team of heroes back through the streets of Bradford that evening and held the cup aloft to rapturous applause as he and the rest of the triumphant stars carved their names into the fabric of the club.

Estimates suggest that 100,000 thronged the streets of the city to watch the lauded stars arrive back. After a journey cross country by rail from the North West, the players were transported by horse-drawn charabanc to a nearby hotel to parade the new addition to the cabinet. The FA Cup was in the grasp of the proud captain as he quite literally brought the silverware home – with the Bantams winning the FA Cup in the year that a new trophy had been introduced, a prize designed by Bradford jewellers Fattorini's and a blueprint that was befitting the prestigious tournament.

It capped a memorable term for the club, having finished fifth in the First Division as they cemented their reputation as one of the English game's brightest sides with strong form on all fronts.

The centenary of that most famous of FA Cup wins, in 2011, brought the heroes of that era back to the forefront: celebrated, lauded and, most importantly, remembered by a generation of supporters reliving the achievements all over again. While the sporting prowess of that legendary Bradford team was at the centre of the 100th anniversary, the club's supporters were careful not to ignore the wartime accomplishments of their heroes.

In June 2011 a group of twenty Bradford City fans trod the path to the continent to pay their respects to the fallen. The group, led by the football club's Bantampast Museum Curator Dave Pendleton, was limited in number for logistical purposes – but the spaces could have been filled more than two times over as devoted supporters quickly snapped up seats for an emotional journey that took them back to the landscapes that once provided the backdrop to the most brutal of conflicts.

The trip took the select band of Bantams to the graves and memorials marking the final resting places of the nine men who died on the First World War battlefields who had pulled on the Bradford shirt. The four-day trip to France and Belgium included time at the Somme, where 1,770 Bradford Pals volunteers were killed or wounded on a single morning on 1 July in 1916, at Serre. It was the first day of the Battle of the Somme. On that bloody day the British Army had 57,470 casualties, including 19,240 killed.

In 2005 a similar group visited the grave of Speirs and the scene of his death at Passchendaele. On 22 August 1917, he was believed to have been hit in the thigh and crawled into a shell hole as his company advanced towards German lines. His body was recovered in 1919 between British and German lines and buried in Dochy New Farm British Military Cemetery, one of 1,439 soldiers buried there.

The extended tour in 2011, coinciding with the FA Cup win centenary, provided another respectful nod to one of the most revered characters in the past of a proud club and a city which can also lay claim to the only professional footballer to win the Victoria Cross. The honour won by Donald Bell, who turned out for Bradford Park Avenue, was sold at auction in London in 2010 for £210,000. Bell was killed in action at the Somme on 10 July 1916.

Pendleton told me:

We allocated places on a first come first served basis and the twenty places were taken very quickly. We could quite easily have taken fifty, given the interest there was in the trip, but felt that twenty was a more manageable number to organise. Jimmy Speirs and Robert Torrance played such a major part in the FA Cup success and centenary year felt like a fitting time to visit the final resting place of those two men. It is one part of a series of events to mark the 100th year since that win.

In 1911 Jimmy Speirs paraded the FA Cup through the streets of Bradford in front of tens of thousands of people. It was a day of real joy for everyone connected with the club. In 1917 he lay dying in the mud at Passchendaele. There could be no starker contrast.

Research uncovered nine players with Bradford connections, either past or present at the outbreak of the war, who died. That number included reserves George Draycott, Ernest Goodwin and Harry Potter as well as amateur defender Gerald Kirk. England internationals Evelyn Lintott and Jimmy Conlin, the first Bradford player to be capped, also died along with James Comrie and the Scottish duo of Torrance and Speirs.

It sounds like a horrendous burden for one club to shoulder, but Pendleton rightly points out that the pain was shared. He said:

When you talk of nine players dying, it sounds like a terrible amount. What you have to take into account is that not all of them were members of the team at that time, so it was not a case of Bradford suffering more than other teams or having an entire side killed. Some of those men had already moved on before they went on to serve in the war while others were reserves. Every team and every town and city bore the brunt in one way or another.

Bradford still holds Speirs in high esteem and in 2011, a full 100 years after the club's greatest triumph, the passion for the former Rangers man burnt brighter than ever as the Bantams set about commemorating their cup triumph in wonderful style. Pendleton's book, *Glorious 1911*, flew off shelves in the city's stores and the exhibition he helped to pull together in honour of the occasion proved to be a roaring success. Line after line of eager visitors filed through and soaked up the rays of nostalgia emanating from the lovingly compiled collection. For Pendleton, the reasons are simple and are twofold.

He said:

I think it reflects on the affection there is for that team – and for the fact we have won nothing since. In all seriousness, even if we had won trophy after trophy after 1911 I think there would still be nostalgia for that very first major success. There is a general fascination with the Victorian and Edwardian era, particularly in this area. Bradford as a city had its heyday during that period and the streets we walk around today, all of those magnificent old buildings, date back to that time. There will always be that lasting link to that era.

Pendleton is a rail worker by day but he has a qualified historical background, a passion he can indulge with his involvement in Bradford's museum and his work to keep the achievements, and tribulations, of the past fresh in the memory of the Yorkshire town's football fans. He studied for an MA degree in history and specialised in the Victorian and Edwardian period which proved so fruitful for his beloved team. It is an expertise that has proved to be hugely beneficial to the club during the period he has been at the forefront of various heritage projects connected to the Bantams.

He said:

In 2003 we marked the club's centenary and that was the catalyst for a lot that has been done since then. I have been the editor of the Bradford fanzine for several years and my involvement had grown from there. We are fortunate to have a real supporter involvement at the club. We had gone into administration in 2002 – so knew the club was in no position to do anything for the centenary the following year. At that time you also had the impression that those in charge of the club had no real feeling for just how much the club means to the people of the city.

In 2003, at the Bradford Industrial Museum we gathered together more than 400 exhibits to mark the centenary. The exhibition brought in more than 10,000 visitors and the great feeling was to keep the collection together. People perhaps knew that we had won the FA Cup – but it is about more than winning trophies and the exhibition was a fantastic way of exploring all of the different elements of the club. We were lucky in a sense that the club had built an enormous shop during the time we were in the Premier League. By 2005 we had been relegated to League One, the third tier, and that space was largely redundant.

The chairman said we could use the space and create a permanent museum on the condition that it didn't cost the club anything. For the 2011 exhibition we linked up again with the industrial museum. We needed them to facilitate it; with the six FA Cup winners' medals we gathered together there would have been no way we could have afforded the insurance bill. Jimmy Speirs' medal alone sold for £27,000 when it was auctioned in 2003.

The story behind the unearthing of Speirs' memento from his finest sporting hour and a half is a graphic illustration of how far the branches of the family trees of Scotland's military heroes have now spread. In turn, the heirlooms have been scattered and only rarely are being brought back together in context. The passage of time makes the discovery of those gems all the more gratifying.

Pendleton explained:

The FA Cup medal had ended up in Canada when members of the Speirs family had emigrated, like so many Scots did in the last century. It was one of the Bradford supporters who spotted it, on ebay of all places. One of Jimmy's great-granddaughters had posted it for sale. Our man got in touch and advised her to take it off ebay and sell it through more traditional channels at Sothebys – and the £27,000 windfall was the reward. I always joked that he should have been on commission.

The medal was bought by Mark Lawn, who is now our chairman but at the time was a fan who travelled on the supporters' buses like all the rest of us. He was just an ordinary lad who had done well for himself – but it wasn't until he spent £27,000 on the medal that I realised he was quite that well off. When he went a step further and bought the club then we knew he had serious money.

Bringing the medal 'home' to Bradford was a nice touch by Lawn. So too was the generous bid that ensured the former captain's descendants benefited substantially from their famous ancestor's exploits on the football field. Speirs was part of a generation of players who lived a very different life from the modern superstars, a modest existence built on a love of the game rather than fast living.

Pendleton said:

We have been able to trace Jimmy Speirs' address and get a better picture of the man. He lived with his family in a very average terraced house on the tramway in Bradford. They were ordinary men, like you or I, and far removed from the stars we read so much about in football today.

I have been contacted in the past by national newspapers attempting to draw comparisons between a player like Speirs and someone like Wayne Rooney, the intention obviously to reflect none too favourably on the modern players. I have always turned away requests of that nature because I just don't think it is fair. They were very different times, not just for football players but for every section of society and you could just as easily compare anyone in any walk of life between then and now and come up with a similar theme.

Finance is just a tiny part of what separates the players of the beginning of the last century from those of the present day. The impact of the war years had a far greater impact than money, or lack of it, ever could.

Pendleton said:

Visiting the cemeteries and memorials is a very humbling experience. Bradford as a club has endured many difficult times. The war was one of them and of course in 1985 there was the fire disaster at the stadium. In my opinion, particularly for my generation, there has always been an ability among our supporters to be able to take a step back and put football in its proper context. There have been far more important and sobering events that have taken place over the years than any game of football.

I've been to Ypres before. I work on the railways so the free travel I get means it is easy enough to get around. I studied for an MA in history, so it has always been a subject that interests me enormously. I specialised in the Edwardian and Victorian era. We wanted to visit all of the last resting places of the Bradford players. Although there are nine names, not all of them had the type of central role that Speirs and Torrance did. Some were reserve players and others had left before they served in the war. Still, they were all part of the Bradford family and to be able to pay our respects to them is important.

For Speirs, who played close to 100 games for the club, the cup win proved, not surprisingly, to be the pinnacle of his career in Bradford colours. In December 1912, just over a year after the cup final glory, he was sold to Yorkshire rivals Leeds City for a fee reported to be in the region of £1,400. It was one of the most significant deals of the era, with Leeds determined to land a player who had proved such an inspiration for their near neighbours in his short time in the English game.

He was recruited by Herbert Chapman, the same man who had put such faith in Walter Tull when he had been in charge at Northampton Town. Speirs was held in similar regard and was installed as captain of the Elland Road side, finding himself in a team that was being built to win the club promotion from the Second Division. It had been a step down to make the short hop to the new club, but it did not represent a lack of ambition at a time when Leeds were mounting a concerted effort to climb the league ladder.

Their new Scottish star and FA Cup winning hero became a regular scorer for his team, hitting double figures in each of his three seasons as the crowds began to turn out to watch Chapman's new-look side.

Leeds City, the precursor to Leeds United, had endured a turbulent start to life and were yet to emerge as a force in the game. By spending big on players who had been over the course, the hope was that a place in the top flight would become a reality. That objective could not be met before war interrupted Speirs' Leeds tenure, with the closest call coming in the 1913/14 campaign when Notts County, Arsenal and Bradford Park Avenue eventually claimed the three promotion places.

After completing the 1914/15 season, with the war already raging, football was pushed to one side. Speirs left his life in Yorkshire behind and returned to Scotland to enlist with the Cameron Highlanders, being posted to Inverness with his new regiment to prepare for a new and selfless life in uniform.

On first inspection, the fact Speirs had to travel far from his familiar Glasgow turf to ignite his football career is an oddity. When you consider the limitations of travel and communication in the early part of the twentieth century, it seems unusual for a small provincial side in England to be casting its net so far north in the search for talent. In actual fact, look more closely at Bradford's history and you discover a club steeped in Scottish tradition from its earliest beginnings in 1903 when the Bantams persuaded the game's administrators to award them a place among England's emerging names.

The first three managers entrusted with guiding Bradford through the formative years were Scottish, a trend started with the appointment of Robert Campbell, who had cut his managerial teeth with Sunderland and Bristol City, at the very beginning of the journey. The Renton-born man was succeeded by Peter O'Rourke, who led the team from 1905 through to 1921 and was the mastermind behind the FA Cup success.

O'Rourke's roots were in the East Ayrshire village of Newmilns and his playing career, like Speirs, had started with an Old Firm experience before taking him south.

O'Rourke, a Scottish junior international in his early days, had served with Celtic before seeing service with Burnley and Lincoln City, also featuring for Third Lanark and Chesterfield before his appointment as mentor to Bradford's fledgling team.

O'Rourke led the Bantams to success in the Second Division in 1908 before his cup highlight, and was briefly reintroduced to the Scottish game by Dundee Hibernian, the precursor to Dundee United, late in 1922. He had a short spell on Tayside before returning to England to take the reins at Bradford Park Avenue, Bradford City for a second spell and then Walsall and Llanelli in Wales prior to his retirement in 1933.

O'Rourke, who was succeeded by Fifer David Menzies, a product of Raith Rovers, made a conscious decision to look north when it came to building a team fit to establish Bradford as a genuine force to be reckoned with. In addition to Speirs and Torrance, a succession of men made the move to Yorkshire to join a revolution that was gathering pace under the shrewd stewardship of the Scot at the helm. Even in those days the attraction of the English game was significant.

Bantams historian Dave Pendleton added:

We had a Scottish manager in the early part of the century in Peter O'Rourke. The club itself was only formed in 1903 so the infrastructure was still all new. Like so many of the northern English clubs, we turned to Scottish players. It was obviously a league that the manager knew and a good source of talent. The team in those early years consisted of seven Scots, two Irishmen and two English players. There is a fantastic story about the team's journey back to Bradford with the cup. The Lord Mayor gave a great speech preaching the virtues of English sporting values – this was a German Jewish mayor addressing a team mainly comprised of Scottish players in front of their German chairman.

With the eclectic make-up of that group of players, team spirit was strong. During his time south of the border, Speirs had struck up a great understanding with fellow Scottish player Robert Torrance. The two men had an obvious connection, hailing from the same part of the world, and found themselves serving together during an era of success at Bradford. Another Glaswegian, Torrance had been spotted by Bradford while playing for home town team Kirkintilloch Harp. The apprentice boat builder had been signed two years prior to Speirs and was well on his way to winning over the supporters by the time his compatriot arrived to extend the tartan connection. Torrance, a strong and talented defender of great repute during his six seasons as a professional, was credited with a man of the match performance in the 1911 cup final. Signed for the princely sum of five pounds from his junior side, the Scot had started out as a full back before moving into the centre of the back line. He settled in Yorkshire and married while south of the border, hoping for a long and happy family life. As for so many of his era, a very different future was mapped out.

Torrance would follow Speirs into action in the Great War and lost his life while serving as a gunner with the Royal Field Artillery. He found himself serving side by side with men who had once cheered him from the football terraces, but his sporting past was merely a detail, noted and observed but only as a footnote. It was reported in some quarters that the defender had been inspired to volunteer after learning of the death of his great friend Speirs. While it was a romantic and heart-rending notion, the dates do not back up the story since both men were alive and well when Torrance made the decision in the spring of 1917. Whatever the motivation behind his choice, Torrance paid the ultimate price. On 24 April 1918 he was killed in action. He and his comrades in the 162nd Brigade of the Royal Airfield Artillery fought in the Battle of Merville as they stoically bid to prevent the Germans from breaking forward towards the Belgian town of Ypres. Days later, on 24 April at the nearby Hallebast Cross-roads, Torrance was among a large group of casualties under heavy artillery fire. He is understood to have lost an arm as a result. The former football star died later that day, although reports as to the exact circumstances are conflicting. Some suggest he died of his wounds on the battlefield while others claim he was killed when shells rained down on a field hospital he was being treated at. There is no marked grave for Torrance, with many men from his battery buried at Klein-Vierstraat in Belgium. There are 804 First World War casualties buried at Klein-Vierstraat and 109 of those are unidentified. Torrance's name can be found nearby on the Tyne Cot Memorial to the Missing, close to Ypres, having been added in 1930. Unveiled in 1927, the memorial now bears the names of some 35,000 officers and men whose graves are not known.

For the Speirs family, at home in Scotland awaiting news of their loved one, there was the small consolation of the fact his body had been recovered and afforded the dignity of a formal burial.

The sad end was a contrast to the typically bullish spirit with which Speirs had joined the war effort as a volunteer in May 1915. By then he and his wife had returned to live in Pollok-shields with their young son and daughter and it was with the Queen's Own Cameron Highlanders that Speirs took his first step into military life with the regiment's 3rd Battalion. He was sent north to the Cameron Barracks in Inverness to be kitted out and then moved on to his station at Invergordon for army training. There was still the opportunity to indulge his passion for football and at the age of twenty-nine the powerfully built defender was still at the peak of his sporting powers.

Speirs starred in the newly formed regimental football team, which perhaps not surprisingly quickly established a reputation for a stingy defence.

His leadership on the pitch was matched in army surround-ings and Speirs was promoted to Lance Corporal within months of joining the army. By March 1916 he had been posted to France with the 7th Battalion of the regiment, joining the others in the

44th Brigade attached to the 15th (Scottish) Division in which Finlay Speedie had also fought.

There was another rapid promotion for Speirs, who became a Corporal in July of his first year on the continent, but the realities of the situation he found himself in were soon forced home. In the closing months of 1916 Speirs was reported to have been wounded in action, although he quickly recovered to rejoin his colleagues in action in time for the Second Battle of Arras in the spring of 1917 and then on to Simincourt and Grand Rullecourt. In May that year Speirs was recommended for the Military Medal, although the citation detailing the act he received the honour for has never been uncovered.

What evidence does exist points towards his bravery coming amid the bloodshed at Arras. Reports of the time outlined the daring of the Camerons, including one ambush of an advancing German line that led to 400 prisoners being captured by the Scottish regiment in a carefully executed operation that relied on steely nerve and fighting spirit in equal measure.

Other tales of the Camerons at Arras spoke of the hostile conditions on the battlefield, with the 'fumes of gas and other shells' heavy in the air as the troops went to work on rutted fields that sapped energy from the weary. Officers said that 'hell's fury blazed from the eyes of the Germans' as the two forces went head to head and recalled the moment when the Camerons pipers struck up a rallying tune to 'send an exultant thrill through our breasts'.

It was in that arena that Speirs was now putting his talents to use and his rise through the ranks continued with promotion to the role of Sergeant in June 1917. He was granted leave that summer for a brief return to familiar surroundings in Glasgow, Leeds and Bradford – not realising it would be his last sight of home soil.

On 20 August, by which time he was back on the frontline, his

Battalion was on duty at Pommern Redoubt during the Battle of Passchendaele. Speirs was wounded during that period of fighting, believed to have been hit on the thigh during an advance before crawling into a shell hole to have his injuries tended to for a short time, before being lost in the midst of the battle.

It was in October 1919 that Speirs' body was recovered and the location suggests that he fell victim to German machine-gun fire on 22 August 1917. The creation of the Dochy Farm New British Cemetery following the Armistice allowed for the burial of Speirs and others who fell at Passchendale.

In 2007 the authorities agreed to amend the spelling on the headstone marking Speirs' resting place, correcting it from the wrongly inscribed 'Spiers'. The mistake could be traced back to the same error on his original army registration papers.

As the dedicated group from Bradford highlighted in 2011, with their sombre journey back to the final resting place of Speirs, it is a corner of France that will forever be held dear by supporters of every club touched by the skills and commitment of James Speirs.

4

FALLEN HEROES

No section of society was left untouched by the callous grip of the Great War. As the death toll grew, the reach of the fight against the Germans and their partners in the Central Powers alliance stretched to encompass almost every profession in the land. As that process took hold, the impact on Scottish football deepened and clubs throughout the land were plunged into mourning as players past and present were killed.

For Rangers the interest was broad. Finlay Speedie, a survivor, had been a mainstay of the team during his prime and Jimmy Speirs an important squad man. Others who lost their lives may have been peripheral figures in Govan but their passing was still felt by those who had played alongside them in light blue or watched them from the terraces at various junctures.

Defender Alex Barrie was a Rangers FP when his name was added to the list of fallen Great War soldiers in April 1918. He had signed at Ibrox eleven years previously, spending the 1907/08 season on the books and playing fourteen league and cup matches that term. His solitary goal, during his single campaign in light blue, was in a 2-1 win at home to Hearts.

By the time he became a Ranger, Barrie was already a vastly experienced player. The tall and powerful Glaswegian had first shown his potential as a junior with Parkhead and won the

Scottish Junior Cup with the east end club in 1899. His displays won him recognition as a junior international and brought attention from further up the football ladder.

He stepped up to the senior game with St Bernard's in time for the 1901/02 season. His new team were one of Edinburgh's leading lights and in the decades ahead became recognised as an attacking force to be reckoned with, even reaching the semi-finals of the Scottish Cup. St Bernard's suffered a troubled time after the Second World War and were eventually disbanded in 1951, but in Barrie's time they were a progressive club.

Within a year Barrie had won a big move to Sunderland, and it truly was a major breakthrough for the Scot. The North East club had been sensations in the early years of the English league, winning their first championship in 1892 and retaining the top flight title the following year when the two division structure had been created. By 1902, at the time Barrie was about to be lured south, the Roker Park side had just clinched the league crown for the fourth time in their short history.

The manager who took Barrie to England knew all about the Scottish game. Alex Mackie, born in Banffshire, had played his early football in Aberdeen and also served in Inverness before treading the path south of Hadrian's Wall to embark on a successful career in charge of Sunderland. After leaving Roker Park in 1905, Mackie also managed Middlesbrough.

The departure of the top man led to a change in fortunes for Barrie, who found himself on his way back to his home country after five years on Wearside. Rangers manager William Wilton made his move and secured the services of a reliable performer with a strong reputation.

The 1907/08 season was not a roaring success for Rangers, with the club finishing third behind Celtic and runners-up Falkirk. Wilton's men were only five points off the pace and had closed the deficit from the previous campaign, when Celtic had a ten-point margin over their Old Firm rivals.

Barrie, a committed defender with noted aerial ability, was not viewed as a long-term solution to the problem of overtaking the Hoops and in the summer of 1908 he was allowed to move on to Kilmarnock. He was installed as captain at Rugby Park and quickly raced through the 100 games mark with the Ayrshire side, spending four years on the west coast before joining Abercorn during the 1912/13 season.

War would soon put football in the shade and Barrie was one of those who would have his name added to the list of fallen soldiers. He was a forty-year-old when he perished on the first day of October in 1918. The tragedy of Barrie's death is that it came after the Germans had effectively conceded defeat, with commander Erich Ludendorff informing his government on 29 September that year that the war was lost and advising them to agree an armistice. With Britain refusing to negotiate with German military chiefs, it was left to Prince Max of Baden to form a new government with a view to concluding negotiations.

The terms were clear – Woodrow Wilson, the American President, demanded full withdrawal of German troops from all occupied territories as well as the removal of the military rulers.

The demands did not sit well with the struggling enemy. Ludendorff changed tactic and plotted for a last stand against the Allies, although he soon resigned and fled to Sweden.

All the time the situation in Germany was deteriorating. Economic woes combined with political unrest and an influenza epidemic that claimed more than 1,700 lives in Berlin in a single day at its peak. With medicine in short supply and the country on the brink of collapse, it was clear a conclusion was nearing.

Late in October there was an uprising on the streets of Berlin and Kaiser Wilhelm reluctantly abdicated, seeking refuge in

Holland, to pave the way for the Armistice to be negotiated. Early on the morning of 11 November 1918, the agreement was signed and from eleven a.m. the Armistice came into effect. The world celebrated, but for so many British troops the peace had come too late.

Barrie was among the last tranche of casualties during the final days and weeks of the German defiance.

At the Flesqueieres Hill cemetery at Nord in France, a simple light stone headstone marks the former football star's final resting place. It is inscribed with his name, rank, army number and the words 'He was a gallant child, loved and admired by all'. Corporal Alex Barrie of the Highland Light Infantry, so used to heroics on the football pitch, died a hero of a different kind.

Records show Barrie served in the 2nd Highland Light Infantry, a battalion that was part of 5th Brigade in the 2nd Division – one of the first British formations to move to France during the Great War. It remained on the Western Front for the duration of the conflict and was at the heart of most major pushes.

At the time of Barrie's death the 2nd Division was deployed in the Battle of Canal du Nord, a phase of the Battle of the Hindenburg Line, as part of Byng's Third Army. The Battle of Canal du Nord was short but fierce, running from 27 September to 1 October and was one of the final stages of the war – part of a concerted Allied attack along the north and centre of the Western Front.

General Sir Frederick Maurice recorded details of the battle in his memoirs. He noted:

The British part in the great general attack upon the whole German front was timed to begin in the early morning of 27 September. On the evening before a great bombardment opened on a thirty-mile front, from a point about two miles northwest of St Quentin, as far as the Sensee River northwest of Cambrai.

Then in the grey light of early dawn the 4th, 6th, 17th and Canadian Corps, thirteen divisions in all, of Byng's Third Army and Horne's First Army advanced on the Cambrai front, stormed the immensely strong Canal du Nord, swept beyond Bourlon Wood and Fontaine-Notre-Dame, the extreme limits of our advance in the first battle of Cambrai of November 1917, and captured Sailly, more than six miles from their starting point, taking over ten thousand prisoners and two hundred guns.

By this blow Cambrai was threatened from the north, whereas in the previous battle we had attempted to approach the town from the southeast, where the St Quentin Canal was a formidable obstacle to our troops, and we had in one bound got sufficiently near to the railway lines (which converged on Cambrai and made of it one of the most important junctions in the hands of the Germans) to be able to deny their use to the enemy.

Ludendorff, in his anxiety to protect Cambrai, had been withdrawing troops from Flanders. Doubtless he remembered our experiences in the third battle of Ypres, and recalled the fact that the Flanders mud had done more to check our progress than had the German troops.

The season was already far advanced and there had been a good deal of rain. The state of his reserves was such that in order to meet the American advance west of the Meuse, and the British advance on Cambrai, both of them blows aimed at his vitals, he had to take chances somewhere, and he decided to take them on the Flanders front.

He left less than five divisions to hold the seventeen miles of front, from near Vormezeele, four and a half miles south of Ypres, to Dixmude, and on 28 September this thin line was attacked and overwhelmed by the Belgian army, supported by some French divisions, and by six divisions of Plumer's Second Army, the whole under the command of King Albert.

The success won by the gallant Belgian king, who had seen his army cooped in for four years behind the floods of the Yser, and had only left it at rare intervals, living with his Queen in a little villa within range of the German guns and in a district incessantly attacked by the enemy's bombing airplanes, was startlingly complete and exceeded the wildest expectations.

This success was pivotal in the events that followed, with momentum well and truly behind the Allied forces and the Germans being pinned back by a concerted and determined push from their enemy. The British leaders were desperate to maintain the upper hand and push the advantage to the limit as they sensed the fear of their opponents.

Maurice continued:

The Flanders ridges, up which we had hewn our way at heavy cost in three and a half months of fighting in the autumn of 1917, were won in less than forty-eight hours. The French and Belgians, following up this success vigorously on the left of the battle, swept forward beyond Passchendaele, and by the evening of 1 October had penetrated almost to the outskirts of Roulers, while Plumer, throwing in three more divisions, drove across the Messines Ridge, cleared the Lys valley from Armentieres to Comines, and advanced to within two miles of Menin. Thus Lille, like Cambrai, was menaced from the north.

While King Albert was putting the finishing touches to his victory the crisis of the great battle had been reached and passed. The bombardment which had begun on the evening of 26 September on the front of the British Fourth, Third and First Armies, had been continued on the front of the Fourth Army throughout the 27th and 28th, while the other two armies were fighting their way towards Cambrai.

During the final stage of that bombardment nearly one million shells, weighing some twenty five thousand tons, were poured into the German lines. This wholesale expenditure of ammunition took place during about one-tenth of the period of the whole battle, and on considerably less than one-tenth of the fronts attacked.

The scale of the battles of the Great War were like nothing that had been seen in warfare ever before. Firepower was immense and the damage heavy. Correspondingly, the casualty and death rate on both sides made grim reading, but there was a satisfaction among military leaders with the effectiveness of the resources at their disposal.

Maurice said:

During the war of 1870-1871 the total number of rounds fired by the German artillery in the field amounted to 360,000, as compared with 4,362,500 tons of shells fired by the British artillery alone on the Western Front, and yet, so tremendous had the effect of the German guns appeared to be in those days, that Napoleon III told his enemies after his surrender at Sedan that he felt himself beaten by their artillery. Science and industry have in less than fifty years developed man's power of destruction to an extent which makes comparison with the past futile.

With this artillery attack we reverted to former methods, and the reason for doing so was that immediately behind that part of the German front to be attacked by the Fourth Army ran the St Quentin Canal, which merges near Cambrai in the navigable Scheldt, is capable of taking the largest barges and is unfordable.

With such an obstacle in their path, tanks could not be used to prepare the way for the infantry, except against such portions of the German line as lay west of the canal, and against the two stretches where the canal ran underground, one of about four and a half miles between Bellicourt and Vendhuile, the other of about a thousand yards long just north of St Quentin known as the Le Tronquoy Tunnel.

So the guns came into their own. It was long since the Germans had been subjected to such a dose of shelling, and many of their troops, having come from the Eastern Front, or being fresh drafts from Germany, had never experienced a really intense and prolonged bombardment. The moral effect of this cannonade was therefore very great. It drove the enemy into his deep dug-outs and tunnels, and prevented his carrying parties from bringing up food and ammunition to them.

At five-thirty a.m. on 29 September Rawlinson's Fourth Army attacked the heart of the Hindenburg Line on a front of twelve miles with the 9th and 3rd British Corps and the 2nd American Corps, with the Australian Corps in support behind it. Debeney's First French Army extended the battlefront to the south and attacked St Quentin, while two corps of the Third British Army prolonged it to the north as far as the loop in the St Quentin Canal at Marcoing. This was the decisive day of the great battle and was marked by many glorious feats of arms.

Maurice went on to outline some of the incredible acts of bravery and fortitude displayed by the British troops. Ingenuity was part of the strength, while a willingness to go the extra yard to counter the German forces was evident throughout as the Allied men used the element of surprise to ensure another piece of the jigsaw slotted into place.

He reported:

The 9th Corps attacked the St Quentin Canal at and north of Bellenglise; the 46th Division, North Midland Territorials, leading the men advancing equipped with lifebelts, requisitioned from the Channel steamboats, and carrying mats and rafts.

Here and there they managed to cross by footbridges, which the enemy had been unable to destroy, but the majority dropped down the sheer sides of the canal, swam across, clambered out and stormed the German trenches on the top of the eastern bank. Then swinging southward they surprised the enemy before he had realized the new direction of the attack, and on this one day the division captured over 4,000 prisoners and seventy guns.

The Allies joined together in spectacular fashion that day, highlighting the strength in depth and the unity that existed within the cosmopolitan fighting team. Communication was key and the machine was well oiled as the plan came together like clockwork.

Maurice said:

The Second American Corps attacked the Bellicourt Tunnel front, which the Germans, knowing that it was exposed to tank attack, had fortified with special care. The 30th American Division stormed through the intricate web of barbed wire and the network of trenches which surrounded Bellicourt, and breaking clean through this section of the main Hindenburg Line, carried the village, only to be attacked in the rear by the German machine gunners who had come out of their subterranean shelters in the tunnel.

The Australians, coming up in support, had to tackle these pests without the aid of artillery or tanks, for both the barrage and the tanks had gone forward with the Americans, but they overcame them, and another breach in the Hindenburg Line was effected.

The 27th American Division, attacking on the left of the 30th, had an especially difficult task, for the westerly bend in the canal at Vendhuile made it impossible for the British troops farther north to keep pace with the advance of the 27th, and its left flank was exposed to cross-fire of artillery and machine guns from the ridge, northeast of Vendhuile on the eastern bank of the canal.

Two regiments of the division, the 106th and 107th, had therefore to fight desperately hard to safeguard the left of the division, while the right and centre pushed on to the village of Bony. Later the British 12th and 18th Divisions forced their way across the canal to the north of the tunnel, and relieved the pressure on the left flank of the 27th American Division which had beaten off repeated and fierce German counter-attacks.

On 30 September and on the following days, the yielding enemy was driven back on the whole front of the Fourth, Third and First Armies. On the right of the Fourth Army the 1st British Division had, by the thirtieth, gained possession of the Le Tronquoy Tunnel, and crossed the canal to the north of St Quentin, a feat as splendid as that of the 46th Division on the previous day.

Its immediate consequence was that the Germans retired from St Quentin, which fell into the hands of the French on 1 October. The Australians, passing through the Americans, sent the right centre of our battlefront forward to within touch of the last line of the Hindenburg system, which ran through Beaurevoir. The New Zealanders and the 3rd British Division crossed the canal to the south of Cambrai, while the Canadians all but encircled the town to the north.

It was on 1 October that Barrie lost his life during a period in which the British advances were countered by the heavy death toll. Those men did not die in vain as their comrades carried forward to complete the job they had begun, showing no let-up in their push for victory.

Maurice stated:

By 3 October the Fourth Army had broken through the Beau-revoir line, and by the fifth the whole line of the canal, and the Hindenburg defences along it, were in our hands. The victory was complete and decisive, and in winning it the three British armies had captured 36,500 prisoners and 380 guns. Thirty British and two American divisions with a British cavalry division had defeated thirty-nine German divisions, holding the strongest defences ever devised by the wit of man.

At last after four years of dogged effort the great trench barriers had been pierced, for between the British army and its objective, Maubeuge, there lay but one German line, which the enemy, believing the Hindenburg system to be proof against all assaults, had not troubled to complete. This line lay some fourteen miles back, and its artificial defences consisted of nothing more formidable than a thin fence of barbed wire, with the sites of the trenches to be dug behind it marked out upon the ground.

Maurice's account of that crucial period in the Great War contains poetry and prose that would not be out of place in any of the great literary works. It is perhaps symbolic of the euphoria of the time that the cold, harsh realities of the strategy and plotting gave way for the rush of the freedom created by the huge headway that had been made in and around those final stages of the conflict.

With rhythm and grace, the great military leader painted pictures with words as he summed up what lay before his men on the foreign fields that had become home for so many torrid years.

He wrote:

The victors of Cambrai looked out over rolling, wooded, and well-watered country with something of the joy and wonder which filled the soldiers of Xenophon when at the end of their great march they first saw the sea.

The leafy trees, the harvested fields, the green meadow lands and the valleys were to an army which had lived and fought for four years surrounded by hideous devastation, with the stink of the blood-soaked, battle-torn ground ever in their nostrils, more convincing evidence of achievement than tens of thousands of prisoners and hundreds of guns. The effect of the three great blows on the Meuse-Champagne front, on the St Quentin-Cambrai front, and in Flanders was, as Foch had hoped it would be, to cause the Germans to yield in the intervals between those attacks.

By the end of September the enemy had begun to withdraw between Lens and Armentieres before the left of our First Army and our Fifth Army, and there were signs of retirement from the St Gobain bulge. He was at once pressed by the French and British forces on these fronts, and the battle thereupon enveloped the whole 250 miles from Dixmude to the Meuse.

Foch's great conception had been realised; he had delivered his big kick and the whole German front was crumbling under it. For a time, on the British front at least, the German morale broke down, prisoners were taken from the German infantry in great numbers and without much resistance, and there were signs of confusion and disorder in the enemy ranks, though the German artillery retained much of its efficiency and the machine gunners continued to fight with their old devotion and skill.

More important still, the resolution of the German High Command was badly shaken. There were no men in Germany to replace the tremendous losses in the field, and many of Ludendorff's divisions were reduced to mere skeletons. He had piled up behind his front, for his great offensive, enormous stocks of shell, and of military stores, and had had neither the time nor the transport to remove them. The Allies had captured thousands of guns. The output of the German munitions factories was quite incapable of making good these losses, and he had ample evidence that the Allied factories had not yet reached the zenith of their production.

In September Haig had more guns, more machine guns, more ammunition and more airplanes than he had ever possessed, while the growth of the American army was daily bringing more and more guns into line. With dwindling resources, Ludendorff saw himself faced by three great dangers: in the east the Americans, more numerous and efficient than he had believed they could possibly be, were threatening his communications between Metz and Mezieres; in the centre the British army had beaten the best of his troops in their strongest defences, and he had no more Hindenburg lines to stay its progress; in Flanders the Belgians, whom he had classed as capable only of defence, had won their way into the open and were fighting with unexpected dash.

Lastly, Bulgaria had collapsed, Mackensen was in dire straits and was clamouring for reinforcements to enable him to escape from the Balkans. Under the pressure of these calamities Ludendorff threw up the sponge on the evening of 28 September. The next day he and Hindenburg met the Kaiser and the Foreign Secretary, who had come to Headquarters, and insisted on an immediate request for an armistice.

The joy experienced by the survivors understandably poured out in public, tinged with more than a hint of relief as Britain and the Allied nations came to terms with the realisation that at last the end had come. It was what millions had hoped for but few had dared to predict, particularly given the power the Germans had exerted just a few short months before peace was finally brokered.

What nobody could deny or forget was that the cost, both

financially and in human terms, had been huge. In every home and workplace in every city, town and village there were people who had in some way been touched by the atrocities of the First World War. Ibrox was no different, with many men who had Rangers connections on the list of fatalities.

John Fleming was among that number. He had been given four games to prove himself during the 1915/16 season and made a good fist of his chance in a Rangers shirt. He made his debut in November 1915 and marked the big day with a goal in a 6-0 rout across the city at struggling Queen's Park. Fleming had come into the side to replace the reliable Willie Reid at centre forward and proved an able deputy, keeping his place in the team for the following week's home win against Hamilton Accies before dropping back to play wing half in a 2-0 defeat at Falkirk, the infamous game in which Rangers played with just nine men when three members of the squad missed their train connection due to fog. Fleming's fourth and final appearance was back leading the line in a 4-0 win at home to St Mirren in December 1915. It was not a happy season for Rangers, with Celtic marching to the title with an eleven-point gap over their Glasgow rivals.

Within a year of making his debut for Rangers, Fleming found himself on the battlefields of the continent. He is believed to have been wounded in action at Langemarck in Belgium and died on 21 March 1916, after being returned to a military hospital in Yorkshire.

The shuddering realities of the Great War reverberated not just in the Ibrox dressing room, but also through the corridors of power and into the boardroom. Two directors, William Craig and William Danskin, both lost sons in the conflict.

William Craig junior was killed at Mesopotamia on 20 January 1917, dying from his wounds at the height of the war. His father, whose position as a pillar of society was reinforced by his standing as a Justice of the Peace, died less than seven years later, by which time he had risen to become chairman. Craig senior had originally joined the list of directors during the 1903/ 04 season and served with distinction on his path to the highest office, He had succeeded Sir John Ure Primrose as Ibrox chairman just four months prior to his death.

The Craigs' loss of their twenty-three-year-old son during the Great War demonstrated the indiscriminate nature of the war. Power and social standing were no shield and both Danskin and Craig bore testament to that.

The Rangers family from top to bottom had been touched. Directors joined players who joined supporters in sharing the grief as all sections counted the cost of a war which, for most ordinary men and women in the street, appeared to be a world away from everyday life in Glasgow. Unfortunately that distance was bridged by the drain on young life pulled in from far and wide to make the ultimate sacrifice in the name of protecting the nation.

5

THE GOOD DOCTOR

The infantry, the artillery and the cavalry. All vital components of the British fighting force during the First World War but all would have been far weaker had it not been for the support of another key section of the army effort – the medical teams. The Great War was notable for the efficiency and effectiveness of the brave doctors and their assistants who put their own lives at risk to treat casualties on the frontline.

The most extreme acts of bravery were recognised at the highest level, and Rangers star Dr James Paterson was among those honoured, with the Scot receiving the Military Cross after being nominated for 'exemplary gallantry in the presence of the enemy' in France during his service with the London Scottish Regiment.

Paterson, a two-time championship winner during his time at Ibrox, was no stranger to medals but the grandest of them all did not come from football. With its distinctive silver cross and purple striped ribbon, the Military Cross was a proud addition to any uniform. It was first awarded in 1914 and was instituted to reward warrant and junior officers of the army for their courage, the equivalent of the Military Medal for those below officer level. The medal was retired in 1993 and the cross became available to all ranks.

For Paterson the award came not only early in his army career but also in the infancy of his life as a qualified doctor. He had just completed his studies at Glasgow University when war was declared and he was spirited away to France to put his new-found skills to the test on the battlefields of Europe. He was a young man and an inexperienced medic but he acquitted himself well, earning the recommendation for his honour.

For a wounded soldier, survival chances hinged on the speed and efficiency of the first aid administered. With the severity and number of casualties outweighing any previous war, the efficiency of the British response was crucial to the overall effort. Lessons had been learnt from previous campaigns and the Great War brought a leaner and meaner operation coordinated by the Royal Army Medical Corps.

The medical officers assigned to each regiment were central to the plan and that is where Paterson was called to duty, posted with the 14th Battalion (County of London) of the London Scottish Regiment.

As the title suggested, the Glaswegian recruit had every reason to feel at home. The London Scottish was born from the efforts of a group of Anglo-Scots who gathered to form the London Scottish Rifle Volunteers in 1859, with sponsorship from the Highland Society of London and the Caledonian Society of London. The steady evolution continued until London Scottish came to being in 1909 and by the outbreak of the Great War it had become an integral part of the British army and was one of the first groups to be sent to the continent to go toe-to-toe with the Germans at the start of the conflict.

Every regiment depended on the skills of its medical team, set in staged positions through the battle zone. The most advanced was the Regimental Aid Post, as close to the frontline as was practical and manned by the battalion medical officer and a team of orderlies and stretcher bearers. Their task was simple –

to retrieve and treat casualties as quickly as possible. The aid post locations varied, anything from a dugout or trench to a shell hole. Anywhere that could take the medics as close to the frontline as they could get.

Wounded men would be given first aid before being carried, or limping back under their own power, to an Advanced Dressing Station, set up by the field ambulances a few hundred yards behind the Regimental Aid Post, for further treatment. These were set up in tents or abandoned houses and farm buildings, far from the purpose-built hospital facilities the doctors had served their training in on home soil.

Various other relay posts were in place on the battlefield, with stretcher bearers often carrying men over miles of ground that was not suitable for motorised or horse-drawn transport, leading to the Main Dressing Stations.

Early in the war the main station carried surgical instruments for rudimentary operations, although eventually they were fitted out ready for full surgical teams to operate from. There were also Casualty Clearing Stations, capable of holding hundreds of injured men at a time, ready for their transfer back to the base area. Facilities included the mobile X-ray units that were created for the Great War medical effort.

At the base area there were stationary and general hospitals established, holding up to 400 men, to serve a variety of purposes. These included specialist treatment for VD, for illness caused by exposure to gas and to deal with epidemics. Buildings such as hotels and casinos were taken over to create hospitals, which operated as they would in any civilian situation with dedicated departments.

They had a holding capacity to give casualties time to recover until fit enough to be transported back across the Channel to the British facilities. Given the severity of the injuries suffered in battle, the military hospitals operated by the Royal Army

Medical Corps on foreign soil boasted a strong success rate. Around 37,000 men died in hospital – but nearly 170,000 were treated, rehabilitated and sent back to serve again.

Several pioneering techniques were pressed into action during the war, including American advances in blood transfusions. Medics also had to quickly adapt to deal with new problems, including the use of chlorine gas and other chemicals by the Germans.

For a fresh-faced young doctor such as James Paterson it was a far cry from what he had studied for. He had anticipated a regular career as a regular doctor and in later life would settle down to become a general practitioner, but instead his introduction to professional life was amid the death, destruction and horrifying injuries inflicted on the frontline during the Great War.

He could not have predicted what lay in wait when he first embarked on his training but like all professionals who were called upon it was a case of buckling down and making the best of the situation. It was a selfless time for everyone involved, even if the experiences of the pre-war years told a different story.

At the turn of the century the Royal Army Medical Corps had experienced difficulties recruiting suitably qualified members. By 1904 there were serious concerns expressed by top brass about the ability to cover adequately in the case of war.

In the years leading up to the Great War there had been a concerted campaign targeting medical schools in a bid to persuade students to join the service, either as special reserves or as officers. It did not have a major impact, with an army life still an unpopular choice for medical graduates who had the competing lure of a lucrative life in private practice to tempt them.

At the outbreak of the war, it was anticipated that 800 medical officers would be required. The number signed up stood at far less than that, with just 406 regular officers aided by hundreds of reserves. Newly qualified students and volunteers from the civilian medical staff joined the ranks to swell numbers, initially employed as temporary officers and contracted for twelve months or the length of the war – whichever was shorter. They were then allowed to return to civilian practice.

The French and Germans had taken a different approach, calling up all physicians for service with the exception of those too old to serve. They were left to man the surgeries and teaching schools.

The Central Medical War Committee, the organisation tasked with recruiting medical officers, enlisted more than 5,200 civilian medics for service. More than 1,000 members of the medical corps were killed, leading to a shortage as the war dragged on. The Military Service Act was passed in 1916, ensuring compulsory service once the original temporary contracts had expired. By the summer of 1917 it became clear that any further recruitment from the civilian sector would leave gaping holes in provision on British soil, leading to an investigation into the medical set-up in France and reassessment of manpower requirements. An influx of American medical staff helped to plug the gaps.

As a civilian doctor, the newly qualified Paterson would have been plunged in at the deep end. There was no time to train medics in the peculiarities of treating war casualties – and initially the authorities had assumed that no such training would be required in any case. The feeling among the rookie medical officers was the polar opposite and eventually a number of dedicated training centres were established to help teach the vital skills and techniques required on the frontline.

Paterson's Battalion had first mobilised in September 1914 when it docked at Le Havre and, within six weeks, was engaged with enemy forces at Messines. Between November that year and February 1916 the 14th fell under the command of the 1st Brigade in First Division, taking in the Battle of Aubers and the Battle of Loos.

In February 1916, the year in which Paterson joined the cause, the 14th transferred to the 168th Brigade of the 56th (London) Division in the Hallencourt area before being drafted into the Battle of the Somme, seeing action in the attack at Gommecourt as well as the Battle of Ginchy, Battle of Flers-Courcelette and the Battle of Morval. The latter saw the Division capture Combles. The Battle of Transloy Ridges brought the 1916 campaign to a close.

In 1917 Paterson's Division was utilised in a series of high-profile battles, includes stages of the Battle of Arras and the Third Battle of Ypres. The captures of Tadpole Copse and Bourlon Wood during the Cambrai Operations were also in the war diary and the commitments continued into 1918 during the Second Battle of the Somme, Second Battle of Arras and the Battles of the Hindenburg Line, as well as the final advance in Picardy.

It was a relentless programme of fighting under intense fire for the men of the London Scottish. There was little time for rest until the days leading up to the Armistice agreement. Relief throughout the British forces was huge. For the first time in four years, dreams of normal life turned from fanciful to tangible.

Paterson was a young man who had everything to look forward to. He had left behind what most would consider to be a dream life as a top-level footballer, who also had a dual career in medicine marked out for him.

He was the son of a Glasgow minister who had excelled as an academic and as a sportsman, fast-tracked into the Rangers first team in 1910 while embarking on his medical studies. Although born in London, Paterson grew up in Glasgow and had been a prominent player for Bellahouston Academy. He progressed as a teenager to play for the Queen's Park Hampden XI and then Queen's Park Strollers before being tempted to Ibrox. The Strollers were effectively a reserve side, one step away from the Queen's top team at a time when they were a force in the First Division. The leap to Ibrox was not insurmountable for the young attacker and he was soon knocking on the door of the first team dressing room.

The 1910/11 season was a campaign in which Rangers crossed the finish line as champions ahead of close challengers Aberdeen. Celtic trailed way behind in fifth spot. Paterson was little more than a bit part player that term, making his debut standing in for Alec Smith in a game against Hibs and later an Old Firm derby. Both games ended in wins and a future star had been eased into the first team fray at the highest level.

It marked the start of a decade in which the Glasgow giants would dominate, keeping the coveted league prize in the city for the entire duration as it was shared between the teams who were exerting the influence that has become familiar to all Scottish football followers.

It was not always that way though. At the turn of the twentieth century there was a far broader base of power in the top flight. Although Rangers had started the century as champions, as the opening decade progressed there were title wins for Hibs and Third Lanark to prove that the provincial clubs could challenge the pairing who could already be considered the 'big two'. Indeed, Rangers found this to their cost when they were defeated in the Scottish Cup final of 1905 by Third Lanark and the following season, in the same competition, fell at the hands of the unfancied Port Glasgow in the quarter-finals.

While those results cropped up throughout the decade, by the time Paterson entered the team in 1910 they were growing less frequent. Rangers and Celtic's grip was tightening and the rookie winger was primed and ready to play his part.

He filled in for Billy Hogg on the right flank in the 1911/12 season, scoring his first goals for the club while on that beat when he grabbed a double against Stenhousemuir in the Scottish Cup. He was coming into his own as a player. With no previous professional experience, the young city medical student had taken to life at the highest level like a duck to water.

By 1912/13 he was a regular in William Wilton's starting eleven, able to play on either flank and providing his manager with options in attack. Just as they had done for the previous two years, Wilton's men clinched the championship prize and Paterson was on hand to collect his first winner's medal in a light blue jersey. The Gers had beaten Celtic to the punch with a four-point margin and Paterson's contribution had been crucial, both as a provider and with seven crucial goals along the way in the league. His match-winning strike against Kilmarnock in March 1913 was a case in point, with the 3-2 victory in the spring of that year edging Rangers to within striking distance of the coveted Scottish League crown.

The balance of power shifted back toward Celtic over the next two years, during which time Paterson continued to cement his place as a Light Blues star with his dashing displays on the flanks, before the events on foreign battlefields took over from those on home playing fields.

He graduated from Glasgow University in 1916 and immediately enlisted to serve with the Royal Army Medical Corps. In addition to being mentioned in dispatches when awarded the Military Cross, Paterson was promoted to become a Captain, and eventually temporary Major.

He returned to a semi-civilian life when peace was declared, returning to serve in a Glasgow hospital in September 1919 and was able to pull on the blue shirt once more. He was older and wiser – but just as effective. Paterson, who had to battle back to match fitness after understandably coming back to the fold in far from ideal shape, made the Number 11 shirt his own in the 1919/20 campaign, missing just half a dozen games as Wilton's side swept to the league prize after two years without honours.

Incredibly seven players made it into double figures for Rangers as the goals rained in, with Paterson among them with his season-best tally of eleven. Jimmy Gordon, despite playing the bulk of the year in defence, was joined by Sandy Archibald, James Bowie, leading scorer Andy Cunningham, Tommy Muirhead and Tommy Cairns in that group.

Paterson's medal from that title-winning campaign, inscribed with his name, was auctioned by Christie's in Glasgow in 1995 and raised £1,035, to beat the estimate by £500.

Only the dogged determination of lowly Albion Rovers prevented Paterson, who was in his final season as a Rangers player, from completing a double in his farewell cup campaign. Having negotiated a path past Dumbarton, Arbroath and Broxburn United in the early rounds there was a celebrated 1-0 victory over Celtic in the quarter-finals. That teed up a last-four showdown with Albion, the team who ended the season rock bottom of the First Division having only joined the top flight that term, at the neutral venue of Celtic Park. Any thoughts of a walkover were blown out of the water when Paterson's goal in the first tie was only enough to earn a 1-1 draw against the Coatbridge side. The replay ended deadlocked at 0-0 and in the second replay the underdogs claimed an unexpected 2-0 win to send the favourites back to Ibrox to think again.

Despite that disappointment in the east end of the city, it had been a season to remember for all of a Rangers persuasion. Runners-up Celtic may only have been three points behind their arch rivals but the Light Blues were streets ahead. Wilton's side scored seventeen more goals in the forty-two league outings and conceded six less, won more games and generally set the attacking bar that every other team in the land failed to reach. It was the sparkling away form that was a particular feature of the season, with Rangers losing just a single game on their travels, at Motherwell early in the effort, and conceding a miserly seven goals in twenty-one matches on the road. One of those away wins was a 7-1 thumping of Kilmarnock, a score only bettered by the 7-0 home win against Hibs later in the season. As well as those seven-goal salvos there were two teams hit for six, as Third Lanark and Dundee were both beaten 6-1 at Ibrox. A 5-0 demolition of Kilmarnock at home was another one of the highlights in a season that saw crowds in excess of 20,000 become commonplace on the south side of the city. Glasgow derbies were notable crowd pullers, with the city well repre-sented in the First Division in an era in which the Old Firm faced stiff competition from Partick Thistle, Clyde, Third Lanark, Queen's Park and Clydebank in the bid to attract fans through the gate. Both Clydebank and Third Lanark had finished in the top half of the table. West most certainly was best.

While the lure of football in the light blue shirt was strong, the long-term prospects of a settled career outside of the finite limits of sport proved even stronger. Paterson was, after all, a man who understood better than most in the game the limits of the human body and when he took the decision to leave Ibrox in 1920 he was already looking to the future.

His brother-in-law, Dr J. L. Scott, ran a medical practice at Dalston in the London borough of Hackney and he tempted his illustrious relative south to join the family concern. Dr Scott also served as team doctor for a certain Arsenal Football Club. It was that connection that led to Paterson making an unexpected playing comeback with the Gunners, spending five seasons in the side before hanging up his boots in 1925 due to a run of injuries.

It was the *Athletic News* that had first linked Paterson with a move to the Gunners in the summer of 1920, having discovered that he had applied to the Football Association to be registered as an amateur in anticipation of his move south of the border. He had at first denied he would join Arsenal, claiming medicine would limit his playing opportunities, but there was said to be strong interest from a string of clubs. Tottenham Hotspur were among the other sides vying for the talented Rangers winger's services.

It was Arsenal who won the race and he ended up enjoying two stints with the club, having been persuaded to come out of retirement by legendary manager Herbert Chapman during an injury crisis in 1926. It was a measure of the esteem in which the winger was held south of the border that the club were so keen to get him into their colours.

Highbury, the ground that Arsenal had developed as their home in 1913, was designed by Ibrox architect Archibald Leitch and boasted a main stand seating 9,000 spectators. It was a home from home for the Rangers protégé.

In total he played seventy-seven games and scored two goals for the Highbury side. When Paterson arrived in London with his boots under his arm in 1920, he landed in the midst of controversy. Arsenal had gone into the war years as an average Second Division side but had unexpectedly been awarded a top flight place when the league resumed in 1919 – ahead of local rivals Tottenham. Arsenal chairman Henry Norris was alleged to have influenced the voting to swing the balance in his side's favour. From that point on they have never played outside of the top division, an unrivalled record in the English game.

With Paterson in harness, the new-look Arsenal began to establish themselves as a fixture in the First Division. They finished ninth in his first season, although subsequent years saw the Londoners flirt with relegation on several occasions while ultimately protecting their status among the elite.

During his time at Highbury, Paterson became a popular figure. The Scot was not only a true playing legend, by virtue of his success with Rangers, but also a true gent. The wonderfully twee story of the day on which he was presented with a bunch of daffodils by a young girl prior to an Arsenal game has gone down in Highbury folklore. The suggestion was that Paterson, eager to avoid offence, began the game still clutching the flowers and played on for several minutes before finally setting them aside once a suitably safe spot had been found.

The good doctor was not the only Military Cross winner of his generation at Ibrox, with former Rangers colleague Fred Gray also being honoured for his gallantry during the Great War.

Gray made his debut for Rangers in the 1916/17 season, blooded by William Wilton on the right wing in a 2-0 defeat at home to Third Lanark in April 1917. He kept his place, standing in for regular winger Stanley Duncan, in the next match at Queen's Park and marked the occasion by scoring in a 2-0 win. In time for the following season it was Sandy Archibald who had taken over as first choice in the Number 7 shirt and Gray dropped off the radar as his military credentials began to outshine his football achievements.

He served with distinction as a 2nd Lieutenant in the 9th Battalion of the Cameronians, or Scottish Rifles, during the First World War at a time when he should have been hitting his peak as a Rangers player.

The battalion originally fought as part of the 27th Brigade in the 9th Scottish Division, serving in the Battle of Loos and many phases of the Battle of the Somme as well as the Third Battle of Ypres amongst others.

Early in 1918 they fell under the command of the 43rd Brigade in the 14th (Light) Division in time for the bloody combat at the Battle of St Quentin and Battle of Avre, both part of the First

Battle of the Somme. The division lost close to 6,000 men in those two actions alone and was reformed after those heavy casualties.

The Cameronian contingent of the 9th Battalion went on to join the South African Brigade back in the 9th (Scottish) Division and also saw service with the 28th Brigade in the autumn of 1918 in the final throes of the Great War, helping to capture the Outtersteene Ridge during the advance through Flanders.

Gray and Paterson never did play together in Rangers colours; instead they unwittingly would have crossed paths in the less savoury surroundings of the Western Front. Both, with their Military Cross winning bravery, did the club proud with their individual efforts and will always be remembered as Ibrox war heroes.

6

BROKEN DREAMS

For a generation of players the Great War ran straight through what should have been their finest sporting years. Rather than good-natured battle on the football field they faced an altogether different prospect on foreign shores. Nobody can tell what would have become of that generation if they had been free to fulfil their full potential, but all had more pressing business to contend with as part of the British forces.

Some were already established members of the Ibrox side when they received the call to arms, others had featured only fleetingly before being plucked away to put their qualities to use with gun in hand rather than ball at feet. The speed with which troops were recruited and deployed was immense, with the fighting pool needing regular replenishment as soldiers fell and casualty rates soared among the dogged army.

Among the men who had his fledgling career in light blue nipped in the bud by the war was Andy Cunningham. He made his switch to Rangers after the conflict had begun, coming into the team for the last three matches of the 1914/15 season and scoring a double in the final game of the season as Rangers won 4-0 at Queen's Park. Having already made a name for himself at Kilmarnock, his fellow players knew exactly what to expect from the man from Ayrshire. He had been a star man for the

Rugby Park club and had a reputation as a fast and skilful player who was never more comfortable than when he had the ball at his feet.

Cunningham retained his place in the squad for the following season, one of a trio of players involved in one of the most bizarre chapters in Rangers' history when, during that 1915/16 campaign, he, goalkeeper John Hempsey and Joe Hendry missed their train to Glasgow due to fog and were too late to take their place in the squad for a game at Falkirk in November 1915. While William Wilton was able to call up one reserve to fill a space, he had no option but to send his side out with just nine men. Perhaps not surprisingly the Bairns won 2-0 that day against a patched-up Gers side. There was no disgrace in that defeat, given the bizarre circumstances surrounding it.

Putting those minor travel problems aside, Cunningham proved age was no barrier as he established himself as a potent attacking weapon during almost fourteen years on the books. A remarkable return of eighteen goals in twenty matches, not to mention a hat-trick against Hibs and four doubles, told the story of a talent to watch in his first full campaign. The faith that Wilton had showed in him was paying off.

Of course his contribution was curtailed by the war in the following years, joining the Royal Field Artillery and rising to become a Lieutenant. He was one of close to 550,000 gunners employed during the Great War, with the horse-drawn units of the Royal Field Artillery put to work on the frontline operating, amongst other weaponry, the howitzers that did such damage to the enemy challenge.

Cunningham went to France on 20 September 1917, as he joined the Western Front cause and he was awarded the Victory and British War Medal for his efforts. Both were standard but hard-earned honours for those who served overseas.

He burst back onto the football scene in the second half of the 1918/19 season.

By the time the following term kicked off he was fully back in harness and at the heart of Wilton's team, spearheading the attack with aplomb as Rangers returned to the top of Scotland's football tree. Cunningham hit twenty-five goals in all competitions to top the scoring chart and steer his side to the title.

He was the leading scorer again in 1920/21 on his way to a second league winner's medal, with twenty-seven goals in league and cup. Cunningham made it a hat-trick of championships in 1922/23, by which time Bill Struth was at the helm, and added a fourth and fifth in the following two years. The 1926/27 season brought him yet another First Division badge and he made it seven the following season as well breaking his Scottish Cup duck in style as part of the side that romped to a 4-0 final victory against Celtic at Hampden.

By that stage the veteran forward was in the twilight of his career and, although he had a part to play in the title win of 1928/29, the cup success proved the last major honour in a glittering period for the club and player. In January 1929 he brought the curtain down on his Ibrox performances and moved over the border to Newcastle United, by now aged thirty-eight. He went on to manage the Magpies over a five-year period and also led Dundee from 1937 through to 1940.

During his time with Rangers he had become a key man for Scotland, making a scoring debut against Northern Ireland in 1920, the first of a dozen appearances for his country stretching through to 1927. He scored five times in all. Not surprisingly Cunningham, who became a sportswriter after his time in football had come to an end, is a member of the Rangers Hall of Fame.

While the war had come at the start of Cunningham's time with Rangers, it had loomed in the midst of Jimmy Gordon's sterling service at Ibrox. Gordon, who like Cunningham was also a committed Scotland star as well as Ibrox hall of fame inductee, had been a childhood prodigy in the junior game.

The Saltcoats boy had starred with Renfrew Victoria in his mid-teens and won junior international caps before being plucked from the lower grade to move to the senior game with Rangers. He went on to spend more than a decade as a lynchpin of the first team and won a succession of honours. The championship in 1910/11 was the first, and there were further triumphs in 1912, 1913, 1918 and 1920.

The war had taken a chunk out of Gordon's Ibrox service in the middle of that winning run. He saw action with the Highland Light Infantry and put his leadership to good use as a sergeant with the Glasgow-based regiment.

As a footballer he was recognised as an inside right but played in a host of positions for his club with enthusiasm and skill, including spells in defence and leading the attack. His final First Division title came in 1920, the same year as his last Scotland cap, taking him to ten for his career. Gordon had first turned out for his country in 1912 and was chosen as captain for an Auld Enemy meeting at Hampden in 1914 as he led his men to a 3-1 win over England.

One of the goalscorers that afternoon was Willie Reid, an Ibrox colleague of Gordon for several years. Reid, who won nine caps and scored four goals in Scotland colours, first appeared on the international stage in 1911 and spent three years at that level.

Reid had entered the fray late in the 1908/09 season and in time became the most deadly forward of his generation. The 1910/11 campaign will go down as his finest – with thirty-eight goals in thirty-three games in the championship run and a further three in the Scottish Cup giving him a record of forty-one goals in thirty-six appearances.

Reid, a league winner in 1913, was another football hot-shot who went on to serve as a gunner with the Royal Field Artillery.

He returned after the war to score eight times in nine matches in the 1919/20 title success before making way for fresher legs as the Bill Struth era began in earnest.

The boy from Baillieston was renowned for his cannonball shot and his scoring instinct, making him invaluable to the Gers' cause while he was in the prime of his sporting powers. In 1920 he was allowed to move on to Albion Rovers and with the Coatbridge side he was promoted to become manager before going on to manage Newcastle United and Dundee United.

Jimmy Galt was another of the Light Blues to have starred in dark blue prior to the war. The Rangers star, who featured between 1906 and 1914 at Ibrox and won his two caps in 1908 against Wales and Northern Ireland, scoring against the Ulstermen, was part of league winning sides in 1910/11 and the two seasons that followed. He went on to serve as a 2nd Lieutenant with the Argyll and Sutherland Highlanders before settling back into civilian life and going into business with Ibrox friend Jimmy Gordon.

Tommy Muirhead also served club and country on the field, appearing eight times for Scotland during playing days which stretched from his early days in junior football in his native Fife through to his retirement as a Rangers legend in 1930.

The Cowdenbeath man got his first senior break with Hibs but was quickly taken from east to west when he was recruited for the Ibrox cause at the start of the 1917/18 season. Muirhead had a reputation as a creative force, comfortable at wing half or inside forward, but he also had noted defensive qualities. His contribution to the title success in his first season was limited in number but significant in impact as he netted five times in seven appearances to help his new club along the way.

As a soldier he served as a 2nd Lieutenant in the 1st and 2nd Battalion of the King's Own Scottish Borderers and emerged from the First World War ready to take his place back in the Rangers team, despite being among the men wounded in action.

He battled back to match fitness and it was in 1919/20, another championship-winning year, that he truly established himself as part of the frontline that featured his sidekick Cunningham.

Muirhead was part of the league-winning team the following term and won the prize again in 1923, 1924 and 1925 – although appearances were restricted in the final year after a dalliance with the emerging soccer scene in America.

Football was becoming centre of attention in the US, with five-figure crowds turning out for big matches putting the sport on a par with gridiron in the 1920s. It was in 1925 that Muirhead was lured across the Atlantic as a marquee signing by the newly formed Boston Wonder Workers. Muirhead served as player-manager for the side and used his influence to take Morton and Scotland star Alex McNab with him on a bumper $25-weekly contract. Partick Thistle's Jimmy Ballantyne was another recruit as Muirhead's tartan connection paid dividends for a Wonder Workers team renowned for its attacking prowess at the time. While Muirhead's introduction had been a success for his club, his heart lay not in Boston but in Govan.

Muirhead was back as a key man for Rangers when the First Division trophy was regained in 1927 and landed a league and cup double in the 1927/28 season. Another two championship medals followed. It had been a distinguished and decorated passage of time for the Fifer as part of a team littered with outstanding individuals who came together to create one of the great Rangers teams of any generation.

Tom Gilchrist had first appeared on the scene during the 1908/09 season and scored in the 2-2 Scottish Cup final draw against Celtic that season, missing the replay of the match which was eventually abandoned following crowd trouble. By the following campaign he was a more regular performer, although competition for places meant he was allowed to move on without spending long enough in light blue to collect an honour. Gilchrist was another to serve in the Argyll and Sutherland Highlanders during the Great War.

Alex Bennett was on the scoresheet alongside Gilchrist in the 1908/09 cup final and was another of those who would go on to serve their country in war. Bennett had become the recognised right winger that season but was transformed to become an inside forward in time for the title successes of 1910/11 and 1911/12. He made it three in a row the following year and continued to make appearances through to the end of 1916, going on to serve with the Cameronians as several of his Rangers colleagues had also done.

Dr William F. Kivlichan was also a Gers man, by virtue of two seasons on the playing staff early in the twentieth century. The distinctive name first appeared on an Ibrox team sheet in 1905 as he vied for the centre forward's berth. A double against Queen's Park in a 3-1 win in his first game wearing the Number 9 shirt, only his second game in club colours, did his chances no harm at all. Over the course of two campaigns he made twenty appearances and scored seven goals, mainly as understudy to the irrepressible Jimmy Speirs.

Like Dr James Paterson, the Royal Army Medical Corps found a place for Kivlichan amongst its ranks. He served as a lieutenant with the King's Own African Rifles. He was sent to East Africa to join a part of the Great War that raged even longer that the fighting on European soil.

The Germans had rushed to colonise swathes of Africa throughout the nineteenth century and when war broke out there were fierce battles as Allied forces mobilised. The greatest resistance came in German East Africa, now better known as Tanzania, where native soldiers, commanded by Paul von

Lettow-Vorbeck, provided stiff opposition. Von Lettow-Vor-beck was regarded as a military genius and he succeeded in pinning back the 130,000 British and Allied troops sent to Africa for years. It was not until after the Armistice had been signed in Europe that he and his forces finally surrendered. It was a smaller part of the Great War but nonetheless a crucial one, as another part of Germany's hold on the world was toppled and another of their key players was knocked from his perch. The Askari soldiers who fell under von Lettow-Vorbeck's command had been stubborn and resilient, using their knowledge of the local terrain to great effect during years of conflict.

The medics had an important role to play in a stage of war that brought heavy casualties and Kivlichan lived to tell the tale. His army days in Africa were not the only interesting aspect to his life – he was the first man to cross the Old Firm divide twice.

After arriving at Rangers from Glasgow University in 1905, the doctor was transferred to Celtic. He came back across to the blue side of the city in 1909, although he never made it back into the first team. Kivlichan ended up back at Parkhead post-war as Celtic's team doctor.

In 1907/08, the season after Kivlichan's last appearance, there was a two-game window of opportunity for John McKeown Bovill on the right wing, a man who went on to serve with the Royal Irish Rifles in the war.

When Jimmy Lister was blooded by William Wilton the war was in full flow. He came into the side to play in the frontline at the end of the 1915/16 season, playing through the centre as well as on each wing in the space of just three appearances during that troubled period. The welcome distraction of football continued to pull in crowds, although teams and schedules were disrupted as players were pulled across the world as part of their service. Rangers used twenty-six players in that one season alone as gaps were plugged to fulfil fixtures, Lister himself being called away to take his place in the forces.

Sandy Archibald was one of the young men who had their sporting ambitions stalled by the war. The young Fifer, from Aberdour, had begun to rise to prominence with Raith Rovers in 1915 and moved to Rangers two years later.

He was sent off to train at the Curragh Military Camp in Ireland and it was when peace was established that the right winger could truly hit top gear and once he did there was no looking back.

Archibald went on to become one of the club's greatest servants with his record-breaking 514 league appearances propelling him to a level subsequent generations of players have aspired to. There was quality as well as quantity, in the shape of twelve league championship medals and three winner's badges from the Scottish Cup. Archibald, despite his incredible array of honours as a Rangers player, was not well rewarded at international level over his seventeen-year career at Ibrox. Eight caps, restricted by the embarrassment of riches on the right flank at that time, fell over the course of twelve years from his debut in 1921. A goal against Wales in Wrexham in 1922 allowed Archibald to add Scotland goalscorer to his many credits but it is barely conceivable to think that a man of his standing and experience in the club game, at the very highest level, would not sail into the international hall of fame in modern-day football. But then Archibald and his generation were from a different era, a time in which honour, far more than money, was the motivator for the proud Gers.

He went on to serve as secretary and manager of Raith Rovers after returning to Fife in the 1930s and guided them to promotion from the Second Division in 1938. He took over at Dunfermline the following year and, while working full-time at the Rosyth dockyard, is credited with keeping the Pars afloat during the Second World War with his enthusiasm for the game. He never had time to benefit from the fruits of his labour, dying in 1946 at the age of forty-nine after suffering from bronchitis.

And the list goes on and on, the brave men of Rangers Football Club who flew the flag of red, white and blue in an entirely different context and on a far more important stage than any football stadium could ever provide.

John Clarke, Scott Duncan, Jimmy Low, Tom McDonald, John Bertram Jackson, George Turner Livingstone, David Taylor, John Rankin, R. Smith, Tom Sinclair, James Young, David Brown, George Dickson and John McCulloch were all among that number.

Records, as scattered as they are, may in future turn up additional names and the full extent and valour of the Ibrox contingent will never truly be known. With the passing of each player, another slice of history was lost forever. Each and every one had played their part in Britain's hardest fought victory.

Just as one man packed his kit to head off to fight for his country, another was lined up to take his place on the football field, as a seemingly endless supply of talented players rumbled off the city's production line.

Rangers and the other Glasgow clubs had a rich source of talent to draw from. In light blue heartland, on the industrial south side of the city, the population was booming. Govan had grown from village to fully-fledged town, with its population topping 100,000 by the time the war broke out. The population was four times as dense as Edinburgh, the residents arguably four times as tough and four times as hungry. It ensured the flow of talent was far more plentiful on the west and the success on the park bears testament to that.

That population boom and docks-hewn culture were the backdrop under which Wilton was working, and many of the Rangers players of the era were from local stock. Others came from far and wide to represent a name that was emerging from its fledgling beginnings to a place of power and prestige within the evolving game of football.

The burgeoning base, as much in terms of support as in potential players, was a key factor in the decision to move across the city to the final resting place at Ibrox. In those days Rangers were not strictly speaking a Glasgow club, with Govan only falling under the city's auspices in 1912. Cathcart, Partick and Pollokshaws were among the other new additions, and together they took Glasgow to second in Britain's population chart, only behind London.

The famous TCF Brotchie quote, describing Govan as 'one of the great workshops of the world', rang true. Before the war Harland & Wolff's Govan Shipyard had been born from the Govan Old, Govan New and Middleton shipyards, revolutionising the industry on the Clyde and making the area the envy of a nation pedalling to keep pace with the industrialised world.

Indeed, Govan's yards were the flagship centres upon which the British forces relied. In the summer of 1914 a visit from King George V allowed the monarch to grace Fairfield's shipyard, where the super-Dreadnought battleship *Valiant* was taking shape. What the wider public did not know was that the full might of the navy, army and air force would soon be pressed into long and arduous action. Within weeks of the King's appearance on Scottish soil he had sent his men into war.

Glasgow became a hub in every sense; as a recruitment centre, more than 200,000 men were involved as volunteers and conscripts; as an engineering base the skills of Clydeside came to the fore, not to mention the area's work ethic. Military hardware and munitions were produced with the care and attention that had been devoted to the vessels that had made the burgh of Govan famous. The reliance on the workforce did cause friction at times, with trade unions rallying in the face of what they feared was a gradual de-skilling of the workforce and, in turn, threat to pay rates in the yards. The labour shortage, which led to an increased place for women in the earthy industrial surroundings, added to the air of change and uncertainty swirling around wartime Glasgow.

It prompted Prime Minister David Lloyd-George to travel north to address a gathering of workmen and shop stewards in Glasgow in the closing weeks of 1915. He received a hot reception, jeered and heckled throughout, as he attempted to brush aside the fears of a workforce which claimed to be fighting to protect its future while an army fought for the nation on foreign soil. A year and a half later Lloyd-George was back in Glasgow to receive the freedom of the city, although tensions were still running high as the war raged and continued to split opinion.

The Red Clydeside movement, as the socialist cause of the early part of the century had been christened, grasped the anti-war sentiment with vigour. The disparate strands of the Labour Party operating at that time condemned the decision to go into battle, and rallies, many centred around Glasgow Green, were common shows of public opinion. Arrests were made and prison sentences meted out for the strongest and most vocal opponents. The move to conscription in 1916 only added fuel to the socialist fire, even if the controversial decision was widely viewed as a necessity in the face of the growing toll of the opening years of the Great War.

There were strikes during the war years, including at the Weir's of Cathcart engineering works. That action stemmed from the revelation that American workers brought over from the company's US plant were being paid substantially more than their Scottish colleagues. At one stage around 100,000 members of the Amalgamated Society of Engineers went out in support of the Weir's workforce.

The government introduced the 1915 Munitions of War Act to protect the supply for its forces, which was one of the most essential parts of the support network on home shores. It became an offence for workers to leave their job to work for another firm without the consent of the existing employer. On the other side of the coin, it was also an offence for a worker to refuse to accept a new job – regardless of pay. The right to refuse overtime was also stripped away under the Act, which was used as often as eighty times per day in Glasgow at its peak.

They were difficult times for everyone touched by the war, politicians and the working man alike. Football, through all the dark days, remained the one positive release for the hundreds of thousands who continued to flock to Scotland's football grounds during such difficult times.

7

THE IMPOSSIBLE JIGSAW

Walter Tull's exploits in the Great War have been the subject of books, films and websites. James Speirs' life has been immortalised by dedicated historians intent on unearthing every last piece of his football and army jigsaw. For others, however, the story of their heroics in the First World War look destined to remain only part-told. One of the major wartime events of British history is, ironically, responsible for ensuring details of one of the other landmark periods in the nation's past are far from complete.

The Blitz of the Second World War over 1940 and 1941 destroyed not only lives, buildings and communities but also tens of thousands of carefully collated documents charting the finer points of the Great War more than two decades earlier.

As the Germans dropped more than 5,000 tonnes of explosives on London, there was little hope that official archives would escape the devastation that peppered the capital's streetscape. The Anderson shelters may have provided protection for individuals and families but there was no time to squirrel away the historical documents that are so sorely missed today.

Millions of First World War records have been retained and meticulously digitised, opening a whole new world for the modern generation to peruse in pursuit of information about a bygone age. For every one that has been preserved, it is likely another was lost amid the rubble and flames that licked across London in the aftermath of the Nazi bombing raids of the 1940s.

It has been a source of great frustration for amateur geneal-ogists and professional researchers alike, and even the official bodies who specialise in preserving the memories of the brave men who risked life and limb to serve Great Britain have hit brick walls during periods of their investigations.

Even in the cases where records have survived intact, pin-pointing the correct individual from a fighting force running into millions is a 'needle in a haystack' operation.

Derek Bird, chairman of the Scotland (North) branch of the Western Front Association, is an expert in his field and knows at first-hand how challenging it is to get a clear and comprehensive picture of events of the Great War when it comes to singling out particular servicemen.

Bird explained:

For those who died during the war, it is possible to search for a particular name in Soldier Died in the Great War – which was originally eighty-odd volumes, one for each regiment. In recent times the whole series has been digitised and put onto CD-ROM which enables it to be searched much more easily.

In some instances, where there is quite detailed information about a particular individual, it is possible to find a match – although with most names there are several possibilities.

Of course, the above is only relevant for those who died – but the majority did not. Unfortunately, finding information on the survivors is much more difficult and often, other than mention in local sources, there are only the personnel documents that are held at the National Archives at Kew, although these have been digitised and can be seen and downloaded from ancestry websites.

The difficulty is that approximately seventy-five per cent of these records were destroyed or badly damaged during the Blitz on London in World War Two. Finding any particular individual's record is an extremely hit and miss, not to mention lengthy, exercise.

The regimental museums and organisations hold some aces in the pack, although again there is no such thing as a complete record in the modern sense. Certain chapters have been lost in the mists of time.

Bird said:

Each unit on active service was obliged to complete a War Diary and although the content varies widely, they should give a daily summary of where the unit was, what was going on and details of casualties – although normally only the officers were mentioned by name. Copies of the War Diaries are held at the National Archives, Kew, but in many instances regimental museums may also have copies or transcripts. A series of official histories were published in the years after the war and often regiments, divisions, or even smaller units published their own histories as well.

Research has become big, big business. At the forefront is www.ancestry.co.uk and its boast of 870 million searchable UK family history records. The site has been online since 2002 featuring censuses, birth, marriage and death records, passenger lists, parish records and even phone books. It was born far longer ago, with the US parent company springing up in 1983 with magazine interests in the genealogy sector before joining the internet revolution. Since then it has grown to become a business worth hundreds of millions of dollars. With every additional set of records the worth of the group grows and the huge popularity of the various international sites increases.

In 2010 the UK collection grew to new levels when the four million UK military medal records from 1793 to 1972 were made available through the site. Every medal granted to heroes of conflicts ranging from the Napoleonic Wars through to the Second World War and beyond is covered.

There were already fourteen million First World War records archived at that point, but the 2010 batch added almost 25,000 citations for recipients of the Distinguished Conduct Medal. With subscriptions costing hundreds of pounds, researching roots has become a profitable area for dotcom enterprises to focus on. That's not to say it is all profit and no heart – with sites opening military records for free during Remembrance Week in 2010. Service records, pension records and medal index cards from the First World War were all opened up for the week in a rare break from the commercial drive of the organisation.

Because of the dominant position in the market place, the website has reported a surge in interest from a variety of sectors. With results just a mouse-click away, the world of records is everyone's oyster and the demand stems from those with an official interest to hobbyists dabbling in genealogy. Annabel Reeves of ancestry.co.uk said:

> The inquiries we receive are from members seeking assistance with their research on our website and range from complete beginners to experienced professionals.
>
> How difficult it is to locate an individual with only name and a rough area of birth to work with depends on a range of factors, including how common the name is and the size of the area. Quite often family members have an advantage because they may have greater access to specific information, right down to an address of the family home at the time. Those details can make all the difference.

The site owners have been one of the independent firms to seize the opportunities presented by the National Archives, the umbrella organisation formed between 2003 and 2006 when the four government arms responsible for holding the nation's information came together.

The Public Record Office held key UK government documents. The Royal Commission on Historical Manuscripts was responsible for coordinating the collection of private papers made available for public consumption. Her Majesty's Stationery Office published every Act of Parliament from 1889 while the fourth and final source of rich material was the more recently formed Office of Public Sector Information.

Those diverse collections were pulled together at Kew by the National Archives, with the management team faced with the thorny issue of how to make those documents more readily available. While the headquarters in London welcomes a steady stream of information hunters each day, clearly the internet is the fastest and widest means of sharing the wealth of knowledge packed into shelf after shelf in the carefully tended libraries. Everything from the earliest parchments to the latest digital files are stored – although it is the hard copies on paper that pose the greatest dilemma.

Digitisation of the documents is an expensive and arduous process and not high on the list of priorities for those guarding the public purse. The solution is in private partners taking responsibility for the process, with the National Archives receiving its reward in the shape of royalties for each sale.

Among the recent phases of digitisation was the creation of an online database of First World War pension records, a contract awarded to ancestry.co.uk. Dan Jones, head of business development for the National Archives, said:

These records are particularly popular, but up to now you had to come to the National Archives to see them. It is great that this next stage of the digitisation – which will allow worldwide access to this important collection – has now been completed. The National Archives is committed to making more of the records it holds available to everyone, wherever they live, and working with commercial partners, such as ancestry.co.uk, helps us to do this.

Each commercial partner is invited to bid for the right to a set of records. The winning bidder is offered preferential access to the set of records they have 'won' as well as the benefit of the experience and expertise of the archives' team and assistance with promotion and publicity. The National Archives website receives over twenty million visits per year, but it is through the associate sites that much of the most popular information is made available, providing links to the partner websites. Compare and contrast that to the physical visitors, numbering in the region of 100,000 each year at Kew, and it is clear that the internet is the natural direction to channel energy. When the service records of more than two million British soldiers from 1914 to 1920 were made available through ancestry.co.uk there were more than three million downloads in the first month following the completion of the digitisation.

The licensing scheme has been in operation since 2004 and has proven hugely successful, bringing in substantial royalties as well as sparing the archives the cost of the digitisation.

Annabel Reeves added:

The National Archives hold the paper originals of both the service and pensions records, which are extremely fragile, in deep storage, and microfilmed copies for the public to use at Kew. The National Archives is one of our partners and we share the aim of improving public access to historically important records. We plan to expand the archives available through our own website in the future with additional military information. The military records are hugely important to both family and social history research and we shall continue to append to our existing collection.

Whether it is right that the nation's records now command a premium is open to debate, but it is clear that pay-per-view for the historical documents has not deterred a country in the grip of a genealogy craze. Television programmes on the subject have sparked huge interest in family research while the resurgence in military history has further enhanced demand. The result has been a windfall not only for the commercial partners but also for the Kew management team.

In 2009/10, the most recent financial results available, the National Archives reported a commercial income in excess of £8 million. It is clear history is big business, especially when the archives are benefiting from just a slice of the pie that is being held by the partner organisations who won the right to sell the material. It has not been without financial pain for those firms, with the National Archives estimating that partner companies have poured more than £50 million into the digitisation programme since the process began close to a decade ago. With further records currently being converted for consumption on the internet, there is no let-up in the pace of progress.

The collections, with the exception of the Distinguished Conduct Medals, were initially compiled by the War Office and the originals are now held at the National Archives in Kew. The Distinguished Conduct Medals collection was compiled from citations included in the *London Gazette*.

Within that collection lies Jock Buchanan, a proud Rangers

man who was equally dedicated when he pulled on the uniform of the British army during the First World War.

But is it Jock or John? Is he listed under his place of birth, Paisley, or his residence in Glasgow? Which regiment did he serve in? Of the hundreds of Buchanans who served during that period it has been impossible to pin down the service records or citations relating to his particular Scot's service.

What we do know is that Buchanan was a Distinguished Conduct Medal winner for his efforts during the battles of 1914 to 1918. The Distinguished Conduct Medal recognised exceptional bravery in the field. Only the Victoria Cross carried greater prestige. The medal was replaced in 1993 by the Conspicuous Gallantry Cross, but the brave souls who won the honour remain forever ingrained in British history.

The Military Medal had been introduced in 1916 as an alternative to the Distinguished Conduct Medal by authorities eager to preserve the importance of the existing honour, which had first been issued during the Crimean War in the midst of the nineteenth century. It was just thirty-six millimetres in diameter and engraved with the legend 'For Distinguished Conduct in the Field' on the reverse of a front displaying the reigning monarch's head. As with the Military Medal, awards were confirmed in the *London Gazette* along with full citations. As with the Military Medal, records are scant due to the damage caused to key London buildings during the Second World War.

It means we know very little of Jock Buchanan's exploits during that period, save for the fact he did enough to join the very select band of heroes to collect their own Distinguished Conduct Medal. We do, however, know far more about his football achievements.

He came into the world in Paisley on 15 March 1899. As a teenager he first played his football with Johnstone, the now defunct club that had entered the Second Division in 1912 and competed without any great success until 1926, when relegation to the short-lived Third Division was followed by the disbandment of the club. Giving Buchanan his break was one of Johnstone's claims to fame during the club's short lifespan, with the young local player breaking from the pack and beginning to make a name for himself in the Scottish game with the black and golds.

While his club struggled to make an impact, Buchanan earned himself promotion up the football pecking order. In 1920 he made the short move to join St Mirren to help with the quest for improvement in the First Division. While his hometown team toiled, Buchanan was a regular goalscorer. He was a versatile player who was best known as a right half but equally comfortable in defence or playing up front, and was one of the shining lights in an otherwise dark campaign that counted as the worst in the club's history.

The young starlet was tempted to St Mirren's great rivals Morton in the summer of 1921. The Greenock side had been one of the most consistent teams of the era, finishing in the top five throughout the second decade of the 1900s and, despite local passions, the transfer represented a step up for the new recruit.

It was while playing in Morton colours that Buchanan first came to the attention of Rangers supporters as he led the Cappielow side's forward line in the 1922 Scottish Cup final, and helped his club to a historic 1-0 victory over the giants of Ibrox. The flat caps were swaying in the open air of Hampden's vast uncovered terraces as 70,000 shuffled into position for the showdown, and Jimmy Gourlay's eleventh-minute free-kick goal proved decisive. To this day it remains Morton's greatest achievement and each one of the eleven who played that day won legendary status.

What Buchanan could not have predicted was that he would switch from the blue and white hoops of his cup-winning side to the light blue of Rangers within a matter of years. His rise was steady and consistent, taking him from the Second Division through to the lower reaches of the First Division and eventually onto the upper echelons of the Scottish game. Ultimately that progression would also take him onto the international stage.

After the cup success in the spring of 1922, he spent five further years with Morton as they fought to preserve their top-flight status. In season 1926/27 the luck ran out as the Ton dropped down to the Second Division, finishing nineteenth in the twenty-team league, after another battle to survive. Dundee United propped up the table but above them the scrap to avoid the other dreaded berth went right to the wire, with the men from Greenock only separated from the safety of eighteenth place by virtue of an inferior goal difference to Dunfermline Athletic.

By contrast, Rangers had topped the First Division table that term after an imperious season which took them five points clear of nearest challengers Motherwell. Bill Struth was at the helm by that stage and building a formidable squad, a pool of players in which he saw a gap suitable for Buchanan. He had served his apprenticeship and was ready for promotion.

Midway through the 1927/28 season, with another championship on the agenda, the legendary Gers boss made a move for reinforcements and installed Buchanan in his side following his move to Govan in December 1927.

Long before fitness coaches and sports scientists, football players had to rely on their own drive and stamina to carry them through. The versatile new man was fast approaching his twenty-nineth birthday and it would have been safe to assume the twilight of his career was looming large on the horizon.

Buchanan had other ideas and went on to enjoy the most memorable period of his long career after pledging his future to the Gers cause.

Buchanan played in thirteen of the thirty-eight matches in the championship-winning season of 1927/28 and scored his first goal in Rangers colours along the way when he netted against Falkirk at Ibrox. He had taken the place of Tommy Muirhead in the backline and did so in time for the run to the Scottish Cup final, playing in the last four ties of that victorious adventure. It culminated at Hampden Park, in front of more than 118,000 spectators, and saw Celtic thumped 4-0 in the Old Firm show-down. Buchanan was in the middle of it all, claiming his second winner's medal in the competition and proving there was plenty of life left in him yet.

The sweet taste of victory was an appetiser for the effervescent Paisley performer, who was a key man in the 1928/29 title success. It transpired to be one of the greatest seasons ever witnessed by the Ibrox loyal, with their heroes losing just a single game and winning the coveted prize at a canter. Celtic were a full sixteen points behind in second place and never had a hope of troubling the champions elect, who won the two Old Firm encounters 2-1 and 3-0. Never before had the margin been so great, and it signalled the superiority that the blue half of the city were enjoying during a time in which the fans were voting with their feet and flocking to Ibrox as gates of 15,000 for run-of-the-mill league fixtures became the norm. Thirty-eight games brought a staggering 107 goals and saw just thirty-two con-ceded, a miserly eight of those leaked at Ibrox in the nineteen home games that term. Buchanan strode forward to chip in with a couple of goals along the path, against Falkirk and Hibs, but it was his qualities at the other end of the park that won most praise.

He again helped his club to the Scottish Cup final that term, when he played in every one of the six ties, but there was to be no happy ending this time. Buchanan instead earned the dubious distinction of becoming the first player ever to be sent off in a Scottish Cup final as Kilmarnock edged a 2-0 win. Tully Craig had already created another piece of unwanted history when he became the first man to miss a penalty in a Scottish Cup final and his team mate's early bath after alleged dissent put the cap on a miserable afternoon. The fact Kilmarnock, a mid-table outfit at best, had given their revered opponents such a difficult time at Hampden gave an indication of the competitiveness of the Scottish game during that era and served to highlight how impressive the cruise to the league title had been.

Buchanan's dismissal against Killie did not cloud the judgement of the Scotland selectors, who gave him his international debut just a week after he had received his marching orders against Killie. That gave the Rangers star an early opportunity to lay his Hampden ghosts to rest and it was done in fine style as he took his place in the national team to face England. A last-minute goal from Alec Cheyne landed the hosts a 1-0 win and gave the debutant a successful start in the dark blue of his country. He had club-mates David Meiklejohn and Alan Morton to keep him company – not to mention a thronging crowd of more than 110,000.

Just as he had done at club level, Buchanan had inherited the Number 4 shirt from Tommy Muirhead. Just a year earlier Muirhead had captained Scotland but there was no room for sentimentality as the selectors chopped and changed in search of the perfect formula. Buchanan found that to his own cost as he lost his national place to a succession of right half rivals, including Kilmarnock stalwart Hughie Morton, Aston Villa star James Gibson, Celtic's Peter Wilson and Dundee player Colin McNab.

Buchanan's second and last appearance for Scotland came a year later when he played in the return fixture at Wembley, a day on which his club colleague David Meiklejohn skippered the team. It was not an enjoyable afternoon south of the border, with England racing to a 4-0 lead by half-time. A brace of goals from James Fleming reduced the deficit but a 5-2 final score did not flatter the Scots.

A consolation for Buchanan was the fact he already had another league medal tucked away in his pocket after helping Rangers to the crown in the 1929/30 season. It was closer this time, with runners-up Motherwell within five points, but still comfortable.

He had also pushed his club to the Scottish Cup final, playing in the 0-0 draw with Partick Thistle but missing the replay, which the Gers won 2-1, to break what had been an ever-present run in the tournament up to that point.

Buchanan won his fourth consecutive First Division prize in 1930/31 as Struth's men gripped the domestic scene like a vice. Celtic had run close to wresting the trophy from the Ibrox trophy cabinet, but fell two points short.

It was on the back of that season that Buchanan, then aged thirty-two, was allowed to leave and accept a fresh challenge in Northern Ireland with Linfield. The seasoned campaigner marked his year in Ulster with another league medal and also helped the Belfast side to the Irish Cup to cap a memorable year and add to a burgeoning collection of honours.

His Scottish Cup medal with Morton had been joined by another with Rangers, as well as his four league badges, although when Buchanan returned to Scottish soil after his brief but glittering stint in Northern Ireland he did so at the other end of football's spectrum.

He was tempted back by East Stirling in 1932 after the Falkirk side had won promotion to the First Division for the first time in their short history. Buchanan was viewed as an old head to help aid their cause, but Shire's time in the top flight proved short lived. Seven wins and three draws in thirty-eight league outings ensured they remained rooted to the foot of the table when the curtain fell on a season with few highs. They were relegated along with Morton, and finished six points from safety, while local rivals Falkirk sat comfortably mid-table. All the while it was Rangers who continued to set the pace, pipping Motherwell to the title by three points. The First Division silverware remained in Govan for a further two years before the green and white ribbons of Celtic were attached in 1936, briefly interrupting the Rangers' dominance of the 1930s which had seen Struth's charges win seven of the ten titles that decade.

In 1933 Buchanan hung up his boots to concentrate on building a grocery business. His time in the retail trade proved shorter than that in football, with his death in 1947 meaning he did not live to celebrate his fiftieth birthday.

8

GLASGOW'S PARK LIFE

Just a brisk walk from Ibrox lies a hidden feature of Glasgow's war past, but one that for thousands of servicemen and civilians became a key part of life in those turbulent times. Under the green grass and rolling lawns of Bellahouston Park lies the remains of the Scottish National Red Cross Hospital – or simply Bellahouston Hospital as it was known to the generation it served.

The complex stood where the Bellahouston sports centre can now be found and is a quirk of the era, standing just long enough to serve its purpose before being razed to the ground to make way for the development of the park in its current guise.

Its link to Rangers' heartland stretched far beyond geography as the hospital was served by members of the Ibrox staff during the crucial period of the Great War as tens of thousands of casualties injured in action on the continent were methodically transported back to home soil to receive treatment and be helped through rehabilitation.

The Gers' effort came from the very top of the club. Manager William Wilton and Bill Struth, then serving as trainer, both lent their experience and expertise to the Red Cross cause and swapped the traditional surroundings of Ibrox for the hastily constructed confines of the hospital.

Struth's skills extended far beyond his primary interests in athletics and football. He was also a reputable physiotherapist and a dab hand at administering medical treatment to his players when required, making him an ideal candidate to lend his services to the huge effort that had been launched in Britain in response to the growing rate of returning stricken soldiers. A spot of minor surgery in the dressing room was not outwith the realms of possibility during the Struth era, with the multi-tasking team boss able to turn his hand to patching up his players and keeping them fit and ready for action.

When the war began he volunteered for service at Bella-houston Hospital and was welcomed with open arms by an organisation creaking and groaning under the weight of the demands being placed upon it. His physiotherapy skills and those as a sporting masseuse in particular came to the fore as the walking wounded were nursed and cajoled back to health. Many were able to return to active duty after their convalescence, some even made it back onto the football fields that Struth knew so well.

With his knowledge of sporting injuries adapted to cater for the servicemen who fell under his wing, Struth even opened the gymnasium at Ibrox to the injured troops and used the facilities and his knowledge to aid their recovery from the injuries suffered on the frontline. Those facilities may have been primitive by the modern standards of Murray Park, but for those who were ushered through the door at the ground to take another step back to health it was an opportunity to set about their work in one of the most prestigious addresses on Glasgow's sporting map.

Ibrox was, after all, far more than simply a football stadium during that evolutionary period and Struth was far more than simply a football coach. The recovering soldiers were in safe hands in well-equipped surroundings, although at that stage it

114

was a still a labour of love as the manager helped to shape the future of the ground. During his tenure the indoor training area that became a feature of life at Ibrox for a generation of players was constructed under the main stand. It was typical of the man who valued physical conditioning as strongly as he did any other part of a player's make-up.

Struth was an example to all who trod a path in professional sports. He had been a committed competitor in his day and travelled the length and breadth of Britain to earn a living as an athlete. He admired leading athletes and set about incorporating them into life at Ibrox.

Long before dieticians and sports scientists invaded football, the visionary Struth proved to be ahead of his time by inviting Olympic gold medal-winning athlete Eric Liddell to train at Ibrox and provide an inspirational presence. Liddell, a lifelong Rangers fan, jumped at the opportunity.

Liddell was actually born in China, in the northern town of Tianjin, where his minister father Reverend James Dunlop Liddell and mother served with the London Mission Society. He returned to British soil to attend Eltham College at Blackheath, a school specifically for the sons of missionaries.

He went on to study at Edinburgh University, emerging with a degree in Pure Science, and it was while at university that his talent in athletics, particularly over 100 yards and 220 yards, began to become clear.

Rugby was his other sporting passion, playing for Edinburgh University and in Scotland internationals during the 1920s before opting to focus all of his energy on his running commitments.

At the 1924 Paris Olympics he switched from his favoured 100 metres upon discovering the heats would be run on the Sabbath. Instead he contested the 400 metres and the 200 metres, going on to win gold and silver respectively.

After graduation, Liddell returned to North China and served as a missionary from 1932 until his capture and subsequent death. In 1941 life in China was becoming so dangerous that the British Government advised British nationals to leave. In 1943 he was interned in Weishien, a Japanese prisoner of war camp, and died a prisoner in 1945.

It was a tragic close to the life story of the man labelled the Flying Scotsman, who himself had experienced the thrill of performing at his beloved Ibrox. The Govan crowds did not only cheer on football heroes.

Each summer the attention would swing to athletics as the annual Ibrox Sports took centre stage. In his final outing before winning Olympic gold in 1908, Wyndham Halswelle set a Scottish 440 yards record of 48.4 seconds at Ibrox. It survived for fifty years.

The tradition was one embraced by Bill Struth, himself an established professional sprinter before he turned his full attention to the business of Rangers.

Struth pushed the event to a whole new level as he enticed British track and field stars, as well as world-record holders from far and wide, to the south side of Glasgow to display their talents to an appreciative audience spread around the old ground and its running track.

The club had hosted significant athletics events as far back as the 1880s and they grew to become part of the tradition in that part of the city. The two-day Ibrox Sports meet included amateur and professional sections, with a bounty of fifteen pounds on offer to the fastest men.

The sports were far more than simply a spectacle since they pulled in valuable revenue; as much as £5000 in gate receipts from a single outing had been recorded in 1949. However, by then the event was drawing towards a natural conclusion. Struth's death in 1956, combined with heavy football commitments,

Finlay Speedie, pictured in Newcastle United colours, was a renowned footballer and heroic soldier during the First World War.

An undated image of Walter Tull in his treasured army uniform during his distinguished period of service in the early years of the twentieth century.

Bleak, barren and battle-torn. The scene at Guillemont as British troops march from the trenches during the Battle of the Somme.

The legendary Bill Struth, who lent his services during the Second World War, at home behind his desk in the Ibrox manager's office.

Willie Thornton, pictured proudly wearing his Rangers kit in 1952, returned from his army service to play a starring role for the club.

Ian McPherson, pictured here in 1947, was a distinguished RAF pilot and went on to star for Arsenal in the post-war years.

The de Havilland Mosquito, pictured in action in 1942, was the aircraft Ian McPherson spent the majority of his flying time in.

Bobby Brown in familiar acrobatic pose during his success-laden years as a Rangers player.

The Fairey Swordfish, pictured in formation flight over England in 1942, is the plane Bobby Brown piloted as an RAF man.

Allied soliders land on Sicily in 1943. Among the number who arrived on Italian soil was Rangers legend Willie Thornton.

Harold Davis, pictured in action for his beloved Rangers in 1958, is a veteran of the Korean War.

© PA IMAGES

Sammy Cox, heading the ball clear for Rangers in 1952, was a proud Gordon Highlander.

© PA IMAGES

Sir Stanley Matthews was a star guest for Rangers during the Second World War.

Another image from Sicily – British troops wade ashore from landing craft on 10 July 1943 as the invasion of the island began.

Rangers manager Jock Wallace, embracing the Scottish Cup in 1976, learnt his acclaimed discipline during his army service on unforgiving foreign shores.

Musician Sammy King pictured in 2011 with copies of the Penny Arcade CD which helped raise vital funds for veterans' charity Erskine.

brought the board together to discuss the next moves. With the ground reconstruction leading to the loss of the running track, the writing was on the wall for the meetings. A proud tradition had fallen victim to the modernisation of football.

Long before then, during those Great War years, Struth had put Ibrox and his talents to use for the British effort and he was far from alone in ensuring the club was represented well.

Rangers supporters have never forgotten the contribution made by gallant service personnel in conflicts spanning the centuries and remain committed to raising funds to provide a lasting monument in recognition of their appreciation. That will not take the form of a sculpture or memorial statue – instead a more practical legacy is planned. Supporters have begun a drive to raise enough funds to provide a suite of rooms at the Erskine Hospital, the hub of the Erskine charity as it sets about caring for veterans throughout Scotland. The intention is to name those rooms in memory of Bill Struth. The great man would undoubtedly approve of the support being afforded to such a worthy and genuine cause, having himself been quick to give time that was as valuable as money at the peak of the First World War.

His Rangers colleague, Wilton, was also pressed into service at the hospital as the duo joined the dedicated team tending to those who were sent back to the west of Scotland for treatment at one of a network of hospitals throughout Britain dedicated solely to war casualties.

While many patients were transferred to Bellahouston to be closer to family in the area, it also treated soldiers from across Britain and allied forces who were sent north to benefit from the specialist care available in Glasgow. As one of the Red Cross central hospitals it was the base for additional affiliated facilities, lending administration support and other services. Its status as a central hospital also ensured that the sick and wounded from the continent were sent directly to Bellahouston, bringing a wide variety of cases for the medical teams to treat and consider on a relentless basis throughout the turmoil of the war.

Although ostensibly a convalescence hospital, Bellahouston had a far wider role in the rehabilitation of its patients through pioneering surgery for the treatment of gunshot injuries which had been patched up in field hospitals. It became world re-nowned thanks to those efforts.

The skilled medics in Glasgow developed a means of operat-ing to remove the shrapnel remnants left embedded in the bone and ensuring, where possible, that lasting effects were minimal. Incredible results were reported, with some of the patients back on their feet and on the road to recovery within a matter of weeks. The techniques were noted and taken back to North America and other countries across the globe by visiting medics.

The hospital, comprising a clutch of buildings huddled to-gether on the site, was built during the Great War with the intention of providing a base for soldiers to return to on the west coast. It closed in the early 1930s, with patients having been moved to the Erskine Hospital by then, with the intention of creating additional recreation space to cater for the south side of the city's growing population, and provide a contrast to the industrial environment of the Govan area.

Bellahouston Park had first found a prominent place on the map in the mid-1800s when Moses Steven set about expanding his family's estate with the purchase of Dumbreck House and the lands at Dumbreck from Robert Smith, founder of the Thistle Bank. Steven changed the name of the property to Bellahouston House and the estate as a whole took on the same name as it grew to encompass 400 acres. When the owner died in 1871 his sisters abided by his wish to give back to Glasgow and the Bellahouston Trust was founded, coming into operation in 1892, and within three years a total of 176 acres and Bellahouston House were sold to the Glasgow Corporation for £50,000 to form the city's largest public park. Glasgow's second municipal golf course was also created on the site.

In 1903 the mansion house and estate at Ibroxhill were purchased to provide access to the park at the junction of Dumbreck Road and Paisley Road. Ibroxhill House was demolished in 1914 and soon after the changing face of Bellahouston continued to take shape with the creation of the military hospital.

When war was declared, the British Red Cross and the historic Order of St John joined together to sit on the Joint War Committee. The aim was to bring the funds and, just as importantly, the strength of numbers of the two organisations into one team with the common goal of supporting the war effort.

Members were split into Voluntary Aid Detachments and trained in first aid or nursing, cooking and hygiene skills. Those detachments were assigned to hospitals, homes and other centres to work alongside the professional medics and lend valuable manpower.

Equipment was also supplied to kit out hospitals and to supplement the provisions in the war zones. It was the Joint War Committee that supplied the first motorised ambulances for service on the battlefield, introduced in September 1914 to take over from horse-drawn ambulances.

Just as important was the infrastructure being put in place far from the frontline. Temporary hospitals began to be created as soon as patients began to filter back into the country from service overseas.

Town halls, schools, houses and other public and private buildings were all commandeered to sit alongside the purpose-built facilities, such as the one at Bellahouston, and meet demand for beds.

Led by dedicated staff and managed by the Red Cross, there was a heavy reliance on volunteers from a broad-brush stroke of society. From cooking and cleaning to helping the medical staff, as in the case of Struth and Wilton, there was a role for everyone, and no shortage of offers of help from the local community.

While the Red Cross contribution was massively important, the experience in Glasgow was not all a bed of roses. The Bellahouston Hospital became the subject of a public inquiry in 1921 after disquiet about aspects of its management. The crux of the complaints and press reports had been a radical overhaul of the out-patient system, which resulted in 953 people being struck from its register. The figure amounted to roughly half the out-patient roll at that period, with the vast majority of men among that number being deemed fit to return to work after fresh examination.

The issue caused a furore at the time, although the committee set up to investigate found that the medical staff and management had been correct in their decision to slice vast numbers from their out-patient burden.

The industrial crisis of the spring of 1921 led to a coal shortage and an appeal from the authorities for the hospital's management to review its case load. They did so, and at a stroke 300 men were removed from the in-patient list.

At the same time the dependency of out-patients on Bellahouston was beginning to diminish.

Reports at the time talked of huge queues forming at the Bellahouston out-patient department, with the crowds gathering as early as seven-thirty a.m. The inquiry concluded that the bulk of patients were very pleased with the treatment they received, although the luminaries responsible for the inquiry did make observations about the peculiar quirks of the establishment.

It stated:

The facts that Bellahouston Hospital has largely to combine the functions of a convalescent with that of a curative institution, that its patients therefore enjoy greater freedom from ordinary hospital discipline and restraint, and that admission to and resident in its wards are attended with certain pecuniary advantages extraneous to its medical functions as a place of treatment, have made it, in the opinion of the committee, much more difficult to manage satisfactorily than an ordinary general hospital for the relief of the sick and injured.

The hospital was initially designed to house 500 beds but quickly expanded to 1,200 as its reputation grew in line with demand for medical care in the safe confines of Britain, far from the shells and bullets of the frontline. Its leafy surroundings must have been a welcome relief to the men posted there from the earthier environment of the trenches.

It is reported to have cost in the region of £100,000 to build the hospital and equip it with the medical kit required to care for more than 1000 men. It was a simple design, single storey and constructed from cheap and adaptable asbestos sheeting.

Casualties from the army, navy and air force were sent to Glasgow to benefit from the care and expertise at Bellahouston and by the time peace had been declared the patient count had passed through the 14,000 barrier.

The Red Cross handed over control of the hospital a year after the war had ended and it was gradually wound down, with just a handful of wards in operation when it finally closed its doors. At its peak it had been a hive of activity, with dedicated orthopaedic and physical therapy departments as well as curative baths.

Bellahouston had been held up as a model hospital in the years following its construction. It was cheap, well designed, efficient and delivered strong results. All of those factors counted for little when it was time to pull down the hastily constructed buildings and now there are no physical signs that it ever existed.

The final day of treatment at Bellahouston fell on 6 January 1931. By then there were just forty-four patients, who were all found alternative accommodation at the Erskine Hospital nearby.

Just as easily as the hospital had been put up, it was swiftly demolished to allow Bellahouston's modern monument to the Great War to be replaced by the more gracious parkland that had stood in its place before the site had been commandeered for military purposes.

Although the people of Glasgow regained their park in the wake of Bellahouston Hospital's demise, it was not the last time the area would be put to use by the army. During the Second World War the Bellahouston military camp sprung up, with the Glasgow Corporation's blessing after assurances were made to protect the fabric of the park. It was a temporary site, with accommodation in pre-fabricated Nissen huts, designed to hold the men returning from combat and ready them for demob from the forces. Row after row of Nissens, complete with electricity and plumbing to provide the mod-cons, were carefully constructed, turning Bellahouston into a mini village in the heart of the city.

It took weeks for the specialist teams sent north to Scotland to carry out the construction. Each team of six men would graft for a day to put together each hut, digging out the ground and laying a concrete slab to perch each building upon. Dozens of the Nissens were pieced together and quickly filled with men, ensuring Glasgow had a steady stream of new faces to welcome and from whom to learn all about the events that had unfolded over the English Channel. There was no better way of understanding than through a first-hand account, although those visitors proved to be just passing through.

Just as the First World War's facility had quickly disappeared, so too did the military camp. The huts were dismantled, the grass restored and Glasgow settled back down to as near to normality as was possible. Through both wars the people of the city had rallied round its servicemen, the healthy and wounded, but the traumas of those who had experienced at first-hand the horrors of the conflicts would never be forgotten.

9

TALES OF THE FLYING SCOTSMAN

One moment you are a star in the making, experiencing the rush of running out in front of tens of thousands of supporters and dreaming of scoring the winning goal in the shadow of the Ibrox main stand. The next you find yourself in the cramped cockpit of a British bomber flying daring raids deep into enemy territory and leading the Allied attack at the height of the Second World War. It sounds far-fetched, but for Gers starlet Ian McPherson that is exactly what happened as the course he had charted took a dramatic change in direction.

When German forces invaded Poland on 1 September 1939 the response from Britain and France was swift and decisive. On 3 September war was declared and life for everyone on the island was about to change, not least those employed in what might be considered the cosseted environment of professional sport.

Hitler had ruled Germany as a dictatorship since 1933 and the build-up to the war had been long and protracted. Just a year after taking power, he had ordered his army to be trebled in size and set about creating an air force. Those were the starting points for the horrifying acts that were to follow, part of a four-year plan to ready Germany for war, both in a military sense and in the efforts to improve infrastructure with the aim of making the country self-sufficient.

First, Hitler annexed Austria, in spring 1938, and then, one year later, the Czechoslovakian regions of Bohemia and Moravia. Britain and France had been among the nations to adopt a policy of appeasement during that period, but the attack on Poland broke that approach and brought the nations to war.

On 3 September 1939, Winston Churchill stood in the House of Commons as First Lord of the Admiralty and addressed his colleagues and the nation. He stated:

This is not a question of fighting for Danzig or fighting for Poland. We are fighting to save the whole world from the pestilence of Nazi tyranny and in defence of all that is most sacred to man. This is no war for domination or imperial aggrandisement or material gain; no war to shut any country out of its sunlight and means of progress. It is a war viewed in its inherent quality, to establish on impregnable rocks, the rights of the individual, and it is a war to establish and revive the stature of man.

Normal life was put on hold and Ian McPherson's story is the perfect illustration. He had first appeared as a teenager for Rangers in 1939, just weeks before war was declared. When that happened his focus turned to the forces rather than football and he found a place among the ranks of the Royal Air Force pilots as the numbers were swelled in anticipation of a conflict that would rely more heavily on aerial presence than any that had gone before. The RAF were primed for a crucial role in attack and defence and in the young Ibrox goal-getter they had a man fit and ready to play a pivotal part in the challenge.

He joined as a rookie pilot but would emerge from the war as one of the Royal Air Force's heroes of the fight against Hitler and his men. McPherson displayed not only skill and expertise in flying but also the courage and fortitude required to earn him the Distinguished Flying Cross. It was an honour that marked out the young Scottish airman as one of the finest to serve the RAF in the most testing and gruelling of circumstances, with so many crews lost while operating over both German and Allied territory. It was a role fraught with danger – but one that did not faze the Glaswegian.

Air power had been utilised in the First World War, albeit in a relatively minor way. The experiences of that period had led to a surge in interest among all prominent nations in developing the potency of their threat in the sky and in the two decades between the wars there were giant leaps forward.

Technological and engineering developments were key, but so too were the tactical machinations. One school of thought advocated the widespread targeting of civilian sites with the aim of damaging the economy of the enemy as well as the morale of the nation. The other approach was to focus on military targets and specific industrial sites by using bombers in a more strategic manner. Until 1937 the British commanders had erred towards the former, and the air force fleet reflected that. It was laden with heavy bombers equipped to cause maximum destruction.

In the two years leading up to the Second World War there was a rethink in line with thinking that was becoming common-place among Allied countries. These included America, who together with Britain began to place greater stock on the ability to carry out precision raids. Planes were developed with those purposes in mind and by the time the war began only Britain and the US had machines capable of carrying out precision bombing.

They also had the ability to produce planes at an impressive rate, with the simple design and manufacturing process proving a major boon – even if it did, in turn, ensure that the aircraft were somewhat rudimentary.

The Germans were lagging behind, having abandoned their planned four-engined heavy bomber programme at the prototype stage two years earlier. That is not to say the Luftwaffe was not a well-equipped air force, having been very well funded by Hitler in his early years in power during the 1930s. There had, however, been a lack of vision as to the strategic requirements and this was mirrored in the civilian aviation industry in Germany – with a shortage of fuel and spare parts among the frustrations that hindered the Nazi forces.

In joining the RAF, McPherson was, in effect, signing up for a winning team. The parallels between his service in the forces and his fledgling football career could easily be drawn.

He first pulled on the light blue shirt in the disrupted 1939/40 season. The First Division campaign had kicked off as normal before the outbreak of war led to the suspension of the competition just five matches in. While regional leagues continued, with Rangers falling into the Western Division, sporting events fell well down the list of priorities.

McPherson played just a single match in the top flight before it was abandoned that season. He had been introduced by Bill Struth in August 1939 in a league match at home to Arbroath, taking the place of James Fiddes in the side, and helped his side maintain their unbeaten run with a 3-1 win against the Red Lichties. He had just turned nineteen and, as a Glaswegian, looked set to live the dream as he set off on the road to stardom with the club which had spotted his potential as a youth player.

The outbreak of war sent football, in its familiar guise, into hibernation and the First Division was abandoned. When the league was halted just one game after war had been declared, it was Rangers who sat at the head of the table, one point clear of Falkirk after five games with a tally of nine points for the Gers. Struth's team were unbeaten after five matches, the only side in

Scotland with that distinction during the early weeks of that campaign.

But then they were the country's top dogs at that time, having comfortably swept to the First Division title in the 1938/39 season with a nine-point gap over runners-up Celtic. Struth had turned Ibrox into a fortress that term, going through the entire league campaign without defeat, and went into the summer with confidence high that a new period of dominance was just beginning. It would transpire that those hopes could not be tested as the competition proper was stalled just weeks after the action had returned after the summer break in 1939.

Wartime football brought a reorganisation of the domestic competitions and McPherson reappeared on the Rangers team sheet in the second half of the 1939/40 season, enjoying a run of matches at inside forward and demonstrating his goal touch with an impressive run of form that saw him net eleven goals in eleven games in the hastily created Western Division. Football continued to provide a welcome distraction, even if hearts and minds were somewhat understandably beginning to wander to the more pressing events developing over the English Channel.

McPherson opened his account with a double against Ayr United and followed that with another brace against Dumbarton, and then a hat-trick in a 3-1 canter against Clyde in Govan. A two-goal effort in the penultimate match of the season, only a short hop away from Ibrox in an away fixture against Partick Thistle, rounded off what had been an uplifting season in the most testing of circumstances. Only James Smith and Alex Venters, with thirteen goals each, had scored more than McPherson and fellow eleven-goal forward Willie Thornton.

The Ibrox side topped the makeshift league with an eight-point lead over Queen of the South when the curtain fell that year. While Struth's side had been strong going forward, a solid defence was the rock upon which the success had been built. In every department Rangers were superior to their west coast rivals.

The Western Division table took on an unusual complexion, with the likes of Morton relishing their opportunity to mix with the big boys, and responding by rising to fifth place. In contrast, Celtic languished thirteenth in the sixteen-team tournament.

Topping the division set up Rangers for a play-off against Falkirk and it was the men from the west who triumphed, recording a 2-1 victory in which McPherson took his place in the side. While Rangers won the Scottish Emergency War Cup, McPherson was not around to play any part in that run as his airforce career gathered momentum.

The Rangers man was attached to the legendary 105 Squadron and his gallantry in the air won him not only the Distinguished Flying Cross but also an additional bar to sit beneath it, with that second honour announced in the *London Gazette* in January 1945.

The squadron was initially formed in Andover in 1917, but disbanded in 1920. Seventeen years later the 105 was reformed at Harwell as a bomber squadron, flying the Hawker Audaxes in those early days, awaiting their replacement with the Fairey Battle. The Fairey was a small and lightweight aircraft and was ordered in large numbers, with 2,200 manufactured between the first plane's inaugural flight in 1936 and the last plane rolling out of the factory just four years later.

The limited lifespan was mainly down to the plane's shortcomings when it came to the requirements of Bomber Command. Ten squadrons of Battles were sent to France on the eve of hostilities to form the Advanced Air Striking Force and McPherson is said to have flown as part of that group, sent in to lead Britain into war.

It was a treacherous task for the crews of the single-engine Faireys, planes that were deemed obsolete even before the war had begun. Many were shot down by the more purposeful German fighters, but still the Battles were sent into action. During one raid alone, in May 1940 at Sedan, a group of forty were lost to enemy fighters and anti-aircraft fire. Seventy had been sent out, only thirty returned. Those heavy hits became increasingly common and in June 1940 the Fairey was withdrawn from an active role over the continent.

At that stage McPherson's 105 squadron was re-armed with Blenheims and given a key part in the bombing of fringe targets across Germany, France and the Low Countries as well as targeting ships in the North Sea. The 105 saw service in Malta, charged with seeking targets in the Mediterranean and North Africa, before becoming the first squadron of the RAF to take delivery of the quick and nimble Mosquitoes.

Known as the Wooden Wonder, the de Havilland Mosquito was a stunning design triumph. Light, fast and highly manoeuvrable, it had the ability to outpace enemy fighters and the handling to allow pilots to outwit the Germans.

Among the 105 Squadron's tasks after taking delivery of the fleet of Mosquitoes was a heavy programme of precision raids early in 1943. Targets in Copenhagen, Berlin and Jena all fell victim to the excellence of the Mosquito crews.

The men of 105 went on to take on pathfinder duties, marking out routes for the heavier bombers at their tail. On their mission on 5 and 6 June 1944, in the hours leading up to D-Day, the Mosquitos had one of their finest periods when they helped to ground mark ten coastal batteries in support of the invasion of Normandy.

Based at Marham from 1942 to the spring of 1944, a switch to Bourn near Cambridge followed in 1944 as the war reached its most crucial phase. The new surroundings did not win favour with all of the men, the purpose-built facility proving too clinical for many. The entertainment revolved around sport, with football and cricket as well as baseball games springing up. This was in part due to the influence of McPherson and 105 Squadron comrade Kenneth Wolstenholme, who would of course make his sporting mark post-war as a renowned broadcaster and commentator.

Those who flew with McPherson spoke of a skilled pilot and a man who, to borrow from football's own parlance, made his own luck by perfecting his flying art. Alan Haworth served as the football star's navigator. Haworth's memories have been recorded as part of the innovative World War Two People's War project, an archive of memories contributed by the public and collated by the BBC to provide a lasting bank of first-hand experiences from the time.

Haworth recalled:

From January to September 1943 I was on 214 training squadron but after six months got fed up, volunteered to join Donald Bennett's pathfinder group and was accepted. I was posted to Marham in Norfolk to join 105 Squadron flying Mosquitoes using the OBOE tracking device. My pilot was Ian McPherson.

After many weeks of training on OBOE, essentially the transmission of signals from ground stations to the aircraft to enable you to fly down a curved track which was forty feet wide at a known, fixed height and airspeed. The track went directly over the target. It was the navigator's job to get the plane to a point on that track which was ten minutes flying time from the target. The time for release of your bombs or flares could be calculated by the ground stations and transmitted back to us. From my records I see that our bombs or flares landed within one hundred yards of the target on all seventy-three trips I did in Mosquitoes.

McPherson and Haworth became embroiled in some near-fatal incidents, calling upon all of their reserves of ingenuity and character to pull themselves through and live to tell the tale. The Germans rapidly developed defences against air attacks, posing mortal danger to the RAF crews tasked with leading the attack, but it was not only the Nazi forces that turned their bullets on the duo during that eventful period of service.

Haworth said:

If flares were being used to mark the target for the heavy bomber force, they had to be renewed by other OBOE Mosquitoes. If you happened to be in the second or third Mosquito, it was quite dangerous because the German anti-aircraft batteries knew exactly the height and speed at which you would be flying.

On three occasions, McPherson and I were hit and had to return on one engine. Once we had lost our electrics and a lot of petrol. We were not able to identify ourselves when we came back over England and were fired at by our own gunners. Fortunately for us, they missed. We had just enough petrol to get back to Marham.

Another lucky occasion was when we returned from a mission on a night when it was below freezing even at ground level and so the small bombs, which were fitted outside under our wings and which we had tried to shake off when were over the sea, fell off on impact when landing on the grass of RAF Marham (this was before runways had been built there). The bombs were ready to explode. As we were the third aircraft to land we were lucky to miss the bombs of the previous aircraft but we had seen and reported them and the other aircraft were then diverted. In January 1944 we crashed on landing because one of our landing wheels had been punctured by enemy shrapnel whilst flying at 31,000ft.

Those recollections demonstrate the peril faced by the brave men of the RAF during the Second World War. Their part was dangerous but it was also central to the strategy being carefully plotted by the British command. The air presence was not all about destruction and, as Haworth remembers so vividly, the tactical element of those courageous crews was just as important. He said:

Between January and November 1944 I did seventy-three trips with 105 Squadron. Before D-Day the targets were mainly armament (often ball-bearing) factories in small towns which were marked for small forces of heavy bombers. The opening of the second front was exciting. We marked the gun positions on the coast so that the bombers could destroy them. This was 0200 hours on 6 June and I saw the ships and barges sailing across the Channel. After D-Day most of our marking and bombing was in support of the advancing soldiers and a lot of it was in daylight. My last mission – my hundredth – was to Stuttgart.

Like his pilot, Haworth was awarded the Distinguished Flying Cross and added a bar to mark his century of missions. The Distinguished Flying Cross was established in June 1918, on the birthday of King George V, to be awarded to officers and warrant officers for 'an act or acts of valour and courage or devotion to duty performed whilst flying in active operations against the enemy'. A straight silver bar is the further enhancement of the Distinguished Flying Cross , awarded for additional acts under the same terms as the cross.

Taking the shape of a silver cross, the prestigious honour was designed by Edward Carter Preston. Aeroplane propellers are among the details sculpted into the design, with a wreath of laurels also displayed within the central winged roundel. The year of issue is engraved on the lower arm of the award, although the cross is issued unnamed. A violet and white ribbon is attached.

Just over 20,000 Distinguished Flying Crosses were awarded, with approximately 1,500 first bars presented. Honorary awards were made on 964 occasions to aircrew from other countries including Canada, New Zealand and the Netherlands in recognition of their contribution to an overall effort that combined seamlessly with the forces on land and sea to overcome the Germans in every single department of combat.

While Haworth thanks McPherson for partnering him through those trying times, he also has an additional reason to be grateful to the former Rangers man – for it was the Scot who invited him to the party, in the Sergeants' Mess at Marham, at which he met his wife.

The Englishman was just nineteen when war was declared and he volunteered in 1940, following which he was sent to Zimbabwe for flying training. The journey was by boat and train. He spent six weeks training to be a pilot but was diverted to train as an observer, or navigator, in South Africa. He returned to British soil in 1942 and went on to serve with the 214 Stirling Squadron at Stradishall in Suffolk.

Haworth flew his first mission to Essen in the Ruhr Valley in June 1942 and over the next six months performed twenty-six further night trips with his crew. Targets include Bremen, Wilhelmshaven, Hamburg, Saabrücken, Düsseldorf, Nürnberg, Munich and Turin.

He stressed that throughout his time he was only ever briefed to attack legitimate targets; submarine works, armament and ball-bearing factories. He was angered by suggestions that Britain's air force bombed city centres indiscriminately. Instead he and his fellow navigators guided their pilots with expertise – no radar assistance meant 'dead reckoning' navigation was the only option and the skills of the whole crew were put to the sternest test. In 1943 he served on 214 Training Squadron, but after six months opted to volunteer for Donald Bennett's pathfinder group, leading to his pairing with McPherson at Marham.

While Haworth settled down to married life with his new bride, McPherson was to return to the limelight as a sportsman during peacetime. Upon completing his service, it was the midlands of England rather than the west coast of Scotland that became home to the airman.

He spent a season in the regional wartime leagues south of the border with Notts County, a side that had spent the years prior to the war languishing in the Third Division and which remained there for several years to come.

It was a step down for a young player who had served his apprenticeship in the Bill Struth inspired surroundings of Ibrox and been brought up on a diet of ambition served with a healthy portion of success.

McPherson's qualities soon shone through and it took just a matter of months for the big clubs to take notice. He was recruited by Arsenal in the summer of 1946, in time for the restart of competitive action, and found himself in an environment more akin to his early start in Glasgow.

The Scottish new boy established himself as first choice for the Gunners' right wing berth, landing in a side that had been one of England's most powerful forces before the war. The capital giants took time to hit their stride as normal service resumed, although there were far better times just around the corner for the Highbury outfit.

By 1948 the North London team had reclaimed the First Division championship and McPherson was a key man, put to use on both flanks and proving his versatility.

The Glaswegian had gained a reputation as a pacy, strong and potent winger with a cannonball shot – although he could also frustrate with inconsistency, according to reports of the time.

In 1951, after more than 150 games for Arsenal, McPherson was allowed to rejoin Notts County and spent two years with the Magpies. He was joining a club rising through the ranks, having fallen to the bottom tier in the 1940s, but gaining promotion to the Second Division in 1950. Experience was viewed as the key to further progress and, during his two terms as a regular in the County team, McPherson helped the club consolidate their position and provide a platform for regular football at that level for them for several years to come.

He moved on to Brentford, who were Second Division rivals of Notts County at the time, in the summer of 1953 but played just four league games for the London side during a term in which his new side were relegated. Stints with Bedford Town and then Cambridge United while well into his thirties brought the curtain down on a long and well-decorated career for a man who was no stranger to serving with distinction.

Despite his experience, not least at the highest level with Arsenal while at his peak, McPherson could not push his way into the Scotland set-up and retired from the game without a cap to his credit. It is difficult to imagine a Scot starring for Rangers and Arsenal struggling to earn international honours in the modern game, but he was a player who starred in a very different era both on and off the park. His major honour was not with a ball at his feet but as a hero of the war. McPherson died in 1983 at the age of sixty-two.

10

THE RESISTANCE

The Resistance. Just two words, but together they conjure images of daring deeds and dashing deceptions. Every country that fell under Nazi control during the Second World War had some form of resistance movement and those involved knew the risks were severe. Imprisonment at least, death at worst.

Among the number who discovered how dimly the Germans viewed any resistance was a former Rangers man, the Danish star Carl Hansen, who found himself at the mercy of the enemy when he was captured and sent to a prisoner of war camp in 1943. He was part of a growing group who mounted their opposition to Nazi forces and suffered the misfortune of being caught in the process. However, he did live to tell the tale and went on to recount his own story in print when he penned a book, *I Tysk Faengsel* (The German Prison), charting that particular period in his life.

Hansen, an Ibrox hero during the 1920s before returning to his homeland, had been part of a commendable unofficial army. The resistance movement was crucial to thwarting Hitler's forces. Whether by gathering intelligence, taking out enemy communication lines or assisting escaped prisoners of war there was no end to the ingenuity and resourcefulness of the members. Men and women from all walks of life joined together to outfox the occupying troops.

In Denmark the situation was unusual. Although the country had first been occupied by the Nazis in 1940, the Danish government had not officially declared war against the Germans – who had in turn agreed to give the nation independence, despite the fact Nazi troops were stationed on its soil against the will of the Danes.

While the politicians had reluctantly accepted the uneasy compromise, the ordinary people were less complicit. A resistance movement sprung up, with several former members of the Danish army involved. Its role was primarily as an intelligence-gathering operation in the early stages – but by 1943, as tensions ran high, acts of sabotage began to become more common. German soldiers were targeted and assassinations took place as a nation began to rise up in the face of their unwanted visitors.

The organisation was not all about force. Political pressure was viewed as importantly by the Danes, and spreading the word was key to the strategy, with hundreds of resistance newspapers appearing on the streets. *Frit Danmark* (Free Denmark) was among the most popular and circulated more than six million copies by the end of the war.

The resistance was fierce and German forces responded with arrests. The Danish public responded by staging industrial strikes. The authorities made more arrests and the public responded by calling further strikes. It was a vicious circle that the Nazis were desperate to break and in August 1943 an ultimatum was issued to the government in Copenhagen – sentence all captured saboteurs to death or face the consequences.

Not surprisingly, the chilling request was rejected out of hand and retribution was swift, with Germany seizing power, adding Denmark to its occupied countries. In an instant the previously illegal Danish resistance was legitimised.

In September that year the Danish Freedom Council was formed to unite the network of independent groups that had been operating in the country. Stockholm, in neighbouring Sweden, was used as a base. By that stage more than 20,000 people were believed to be involved in acts designed to draw German troops away from the fighting grounds of France and into the more remote lands of Scandinavia. It was a coordinated effort to weaken Nazi forces in key areas.

The second strand to the Danish resistance was to remove the country's Jewish residents from harm's way. More than 7,000 of 8,000 Jews were offered safe passage from Nazi rule.

Denmark was the only occupied country that resisted Hitler's order to deport its Jewish citizens. It was in September 1943 that the Danes, acting on a tip-off from a German diplomat, first discovered that there was an active move to seize the country's Jewish citizens. Until then it had been anticipated, but the secret information gave the confirmation that the Nazi operation was about to begin.

The Scandinavians rallied in support of their Jewish community. With the safe territory of neutral Sweden just a short but potentially treacherous boat journey away, the Danish resistance swung into action.

The Swedes had maintained their neutrality throughout the war, with the Germans allowing the country to remain on the periphery of the war in exchange for economic privileges, including access to the Swedish iron ore stockpiles, and political cooperation. The uneasy balance allowed Sweden to welcome Jewish refugees seeking sanctuary, and tens of thousands of Norwegians also crossed the border after their own country had become embroiled in the battle. Germany appeared willing to allow Sweden to offer shelter to those who made it to its shores, although whether the Nazis were fully aware of the extent of the situation has been the subject of great debate.

In Denmark many Jewish residents, mainly based in the capital city of Copenhagen, were sheltered by sympathetic families, or found refuge in hospitals and churches, hidden from the reach of German troops, while fishermen and other sailors readied their crafts to ferry more than 7,200 Danish Jews and almost 800 Danes of other religions to the safe haven of Sweden. It was a valiant effort, with those who masterminded the rescue facing arrest or worse at the hands of the Germans if they were discovered.

What made the Danish effort particularly notable was the way in which the entire country united to make it possible. There was support from far and wide as the majority joined forces with the resistance and produced commendable results.

Naturally there were setbacks along the way. Close to 500 Jews from Denmark were captured and deported, sent to Czechoslovakia to be herded together by the Nazis. A tenth of those prisoners paid the ultimate price when they were killed by the German forces. Pressure from Danish authorities ensured that the death toll was not greater and that the vast bulk of the deportees survived.

It was during that turbulent year of 1943 that Carl Hansen found himself among the resistance members who were captured by the occupying forces. His crime of 'harassing' a German soldier may not have ranked alongside those involved with the more violent attacks, but daring to even challenge the Nazi aggressors who had turned their country upside down was a punishable act. While so many civilians across Europe had understandably fallen in line with the brutal German rule, the Danes proved to be a more difficult breed to tame, and their spirited resistance is remembered to this day at commemorative events which celebrate, in particular, the plucky evacuation effort that saved so many of the nation's Jewish citizens.

Hansen's part in the resistance initially landed him a stint in a prison in his homeland before being transferred to a prisoner of war camp in the German city of Neumunster, better known for its airbase which housed Luftwaffe planes and personnel during the war.

The airfield had been created while the fighting raged on across Europe, coming into active service in 1939 as fighter crews took up residence there. The Neumunster base was central to German attacks on Scandinavia, particularly Norway, and was also well placed for receiving prisoners being shipped back in the opposite direction. There were frequent air battles over the city, with heavy casualties among both German and Allied air crews. In 1945 the British forces claimed Neumunster and the airbase, liberating more than 1,000 prisoners who had been forced to work at the Land and Sea aircraft building and maintenance factory on the site. They had been deemed more useful alive than dead by their captors.

Hansen came through his imprisonment by the Nazis unscathed, physically at least. While he was able to return to life in football after the war, Hansen spoke freely about the mental scars that remained with him after his wartime experiences. He recounted his treatment at the hands of Hitler's men in *I Tysk Faengsel* in the aftermath of the war. Copies of the book, written in his mother tongue, can still be found today. Its cover features a caricature of a despondent Hansen in the shadow of a swastika, and the process must have been therapeutic for a man left a shadow of the bubbly character that Rangers supporters knew and loved. Hansen went on to rebuild his life and later published a second volume, concentrating this time on his happier times in football and the joy that his involvement in the sport had brought him. His best years had been during the carefree inter-war years of the 1920s and '30s, when his talents took him on a wonderful journey. He could not have predicted where his life would lead him in the years ahead or the terror that would grip his nation and its people.

It had all been far simpler when, in his early twenties, Hansen launched his football career with Danish club Boldklubben 1903. In 1992 that team, better known simply as B1903, lost its individual identity when it merged with city rivals KB to form Copenhagen FC.

While the name may be a fading memory to today's football fans, in the early part of the twentieth century the B1903 badge was a prestigious one. The team, still in its early years, was crowned champions of Denmark in 1920 and Hansen was part of that success story as a rising star of the all-amateur domestic game.

A twist of fate led to his big break in the professional game when Rangers accepted an invitation to take part in a mini-tour of Denmark. Over the space of five days the Light Blues tackled club sides AB and B1903, as well as a Copenhagen select team. The trip, early in June 1921 on the back of a title-winning campaign in Scotland, went well for the Ibrox men in more ways than one as they returned not only with an enhanced reputation after some impressive performances, but also with a potential new recruit in their sights.

On the field the Glasgow visitors breezed to three victories from their three matches. A 2-0 win against AB opened the sequence and was followed, after a day's rest, by a 2-1 victory against B1903. Another day off to recover from those exertions was followed by the final match against the city's select side, which also ended 2-1 in Rangers' favour thanks to an Andy Cunningham double. It was mission accomplished as Bill Struth's charges got a taste of the Scandinavian style of play. There was much intrigue surrounding the arrival of the Scottish champions, with more than 50,000 locals turning out over the course of the three fixtures.

The middle of this series gave Struth his first glimpse of a small and lively striker by the name of Carl Hansen, or Carl Skomager as he was known in his homeland. The Skomager moniker derived from his father's trade as a cobbler and translates as shoemaker. He was a twenty-three-year-old live-wire who made an immediate impact when he lined up against the Gers on their whistle-stop summer tour.

With seven caps under his belt, the forward's abilities were no secret to fans in his home country, but those abilities were about to be taken to a whole new audience. As a twenty-year-old he scored twice against Sweden on his debut for Denmark and had been in line for a place in the 1920 Olympics team until a breach in team discipline, when he was punished for sleeping in and taking breakfast in his room rather than with the rest of the team, cost him his place.

That mild controversy did not trouble Struth. The Ibrox manager decided after seeing the player that he wanted Hansen in his team and the wheels were set in motion to give the Rangers supporters a continental treat.

It was not the most straightforward transfer the club has ever been involved in. With its strict amateur policy in place, luring a Danish player into the paid ranks had consequences that in today's money-centric climate sound absurd. Hansen faced a weighty decision when Rangers made their move, since joining a professional team would preclude him from playing for the Danish national side, and would also make the road to a return move to Denmark a rocky one. It was not until the dawn of the 1970s that professional players were allowed to feature for the country's international team.

Eventually, in October 1921, the transfer was concluded and Hansen made the hop across the North Sea to Scotland and the next chapter in his life and career. Rangers are reported to have paid a bounty of twenty pounds to land their imported star, who became Denmark's first ever professional player. It whipped up a wealth of excitement in his homeland and Hansen set about living up to his billing with some hugely impressive displays.

None was more impressive than his first. Making his debut away to Queen's Park in the Lord Provost's Rent Relief Fund Cup, Hansen rattled in a hat-trick to announce his arrival in the Scottish game. Rangers went on to win the competition, beating Celtic 2-0 in the Hampden final in a match marked by another Hansen goal.

In the more serious business of the league, the Scandinavian hot-shot was no less potent. He scored another hat-trick, this time in front of an Ibrox crowd against Airdrie, on his way to a haul of eight goals in just eleven appearances. In all competitions his return was sixteen goals in sixteen games, which included a double against a Copenhagen select when he returned to Denmark with his new club for a series of games in the summer of 1922.

Aside from the Provost's Cup, Hansen ended his debut season empty-handed. The 1922/23 campaign was more successful for the club, with the title flag reclaimed. Hansen proved an able deputy for regular Number 9 Geordie Henderson that term, scoring half a dozen goals in the league. He continued his Old Firm habit too, netting against Celtic in a 2-0 New Year's Day derby.

A career that had started with a bang, and that debut hat-trick, ended with a whimper as Hansen suffered an injury nightmare during the 1923/24 season. Having been restricted mainly to reserve outings, featuring only twice in Struth's first team, the popular Dane broke his leg while playing for the second string. It marked the end of his time as a Rangers player – although not the end of his time as a proud Ranger. Long after he had departed from Scotland, Hansen spoke in glowing terms of his Ibrox connection and remained a fan of the team that had shown such faith in him as a young man.

While he was unable to force his way into the team on a regular basis, it was Hansen who blazed the trail for the succession of Scandinavian stars who have graced the Ibrox turf down through the years.

As a professional player returning to an amateur league in Denmark, Hansen was left out in the cold for a two-year qualifying period before regaining his amateur status. He returned to his first club, B1903, and played out his playing days with the Copenhagen side before embarking on a coaching career that he launched with the youth team of AB and continued back with B1903's senior side through until 1948.

Two years later he was guest of honour when Copenhagen side AB touched down in Glasgow for a challenge match against Rangers, keeping alive the proud links between the club and the Danish opposition that could be traced back to the VIP visitor's playing days.

The Ibrox old-boy made a beeline for the Victoria Infirmary, where his old boss Bill Struth was being treated. The two had an emotional reunion, with Struth credited as a major influence on Hansen during his time in Glasgow in the 1920s. Water had passed under the bridge for both men but the friendship had never been forgotten.

Back at Ibrox, Hansen received an ovation from the home crowd when he arrived for the match. It was a fitting homecoming for a figure who had been a favourite with the Bears. Hansen took the opportunity to present the club with a vase which still sits in the trophy room.

The Glasgow expedition proved not to be Hansen's final overseas commitment in football. In 1952 he was picked to lead Denmark's team for the Olympics in Helsinki, recognition of the impressive coaching CV he had established while working with youth and senior players at club level. He had a reputation for encouraging his teams to express themselves and play the game in the correct manner, ideal for the Olympic arena.

He took an experienced side to Finland at a time when his

country remained fiercely proud of its amateur status, and led the underdogs to victories against Greece and Poland in the early round before falling 5-3 against Yugoslavia in the quarter-finals. Hungary were the team who came through to win gold but the Danes could be proud of their achievement in reaching the last eight of the competition.

Hansen, who was a hero at home and abroad, both in his football days and in wartime, died in Denmark in 1978, just days after marking his eightieth birthday.

11

NAVY BLUES

Legendary Rangers and Scotland goalkeeper Bobby Brown had every reason to believe that his prowess between the sticks saved his life during the long years of the Second World War. The renowned shot-stopper was one of a number of Rangers men who served in the Royal Navy during that period and was also among the contingent of sports stars of his generation who found his athletic ambitions rekindled unexpectedly during a time of huge uncertainty.

Brown had entered the services expecting to spend the foreseeable future battling the Nazi enemy in the air and at sea as part of the skilled Navy Flying Corps. It transpired his talents as a footballer would see him diverted by his superiors and afforded the opportunity to continue his quest for excellence while serving his time in a navy uniform.

Brown, born in the Stirlingshire village of Dunipace in 1923, was a budding young talent with Queen's Park in 1939 when war broke out. The fresh-faced sixteen-year-old actually got his big break due to the outbreak of war, promoted to the Spiders first team in 1940 at short notice after two senior goalkeepers had been called up to the forces.

He made his debut against Celtic at Parkhead – and conceded a goal within minutes. Unabashed, Brown continued his football education with Queen's and soon enrolled at Jordanhill College in Glasgow to take his first step on the road to a career as a P.E. teacher.

His studies at Jordanhill were cut short when Brown volunteered to join the Fleet Air Arm of the Royal Navy and moved to the Dartmouth Naval College in 1941. Six fellow students at the college joined him in the same service – five of them were killed in action.

Brown qualified as a Fairey Swordfish pilot and became a petty officer in what was a relatively new arm of the British armed forces. The naval wing of the Royal Flying Corps was formed in 1912, switching from RAF to Royal Navy control in May 1939 as the Fleet Air Arm.

The Swordfish became one of the most iconic aircraft of the Fleet Air Arm. Very few aircraft lasted the duration of the Second World War and it was one of that select number. It also became the last bi-plane to be used in combat and was instrumental in the sinking of the *Bismarck* in 1941.

Nicknamed the 'String Bag' because of the mixed bag of weaponry it could carry, the distinctive Swordfish entered service in 1936 and, at its peak, there were twenty-five squadrons of the plane operating during the Second World War. More than 2,300 were built in total and they became valuable weapons in the fight against enemy fleets at sea, not only bringing about the demise of the *Bismarck* but also helping to cripple the Italian fleet at Taranto in 1940 and playing a key part in the battle of Cape Matapan the following year.

The Swordfish and its pilots also served as convoy escorts and on anti-submarine patrols, displaying not only durability in the face of enemy fire but also the agility required to enable its pilots to dodge their way out of trouble.

The Swordfish was just part of the hardware stockpile at the disposal of navy commanders. At the start of the war the Fleet

Air Arm had a band of just 232 aircraft. By the end, that number had risen to more than 3,700 planes.

Air power from both ships and land was deemed to be central to the navy strategy, with the Swordfish capable of operating from the decks of the navy's expanding fleet of carriers. The carriers were specific to the British, US and Japanese forces during the Second World War. The Germans had been slow in waking up to the potential afforded by the carriers and as such did not begin a design and construction programme until it was too late. Britain, in contrast, was busy pioneering the use of technology such as arrester hooks for landings and making full use of the added range and aerial power the fleet provided it with.

The development of the naval air capability was one of the biggest single developments between the wars and the recruitment of men capable of carrying out the very specialised operations was key.

Brown earned his spurs as a pilot among that brave band of men, picking up unique skills in his early navy training as part of a rapidly expanding force that was to be charged with patrolling the treacherous seas of the world during the global conflict. He was a young man sent into the wide world early in his life to slot into the war wherever he was required. It transpired that it was not only in the cockpit that the sporting Scot was set to be asked to put his talent, intelligence and razor-sharp reactions to good use.

He also had the opportunity to pull on his goalkeeper's shirt regularly, starring in the Combined Services team and also featuring in all of Scotland's wartime internationals. He returned to Scotland regularly to turn out for Queen's Park and also guested for a succession of English club sides.

It was his standout displays for the Royal Navy side that ensured Brown's days as a flying ace came to a premature end.

The First Lord of the Admiralty, A. V. Alexander, knew a thing or two about football, as vice-president of Chelsea. He watched Brown's performance in navy colours with interest and enlisted him to guest for the Stamford Bridge club.

Alexander also arranged for Brown to be pulled away from Fleet Air Arm duties and sent instead to the less perilous environs of the Royal Navy School of Physical Training at Portsmouth, where he was able to continue the teacher training he had started in Glasgow. Despite his grand title, the leader of the admiralty was a proud working-class politician who had risen to the position of power through hard work and dedication. Despite his lofty responsibilities, Alexander, who laid claim to the tag of Churchill's Favourite Socialist, had a reputation for putting the welfare of the servicemen at the top of his list of priorities. Brown's treatment is testament to that approach, not to mention to his love of football.

After moving to Portsmouth's physical education centre, Brown combined his studies with his guest performances, not only for Chelsea but also with Portsmouth and Plymouth. The military hierarchy placed great importance on maintaining morale not only among troops but among the wider public and football, as the leading form of entertainment of the time, was not neglected.

After being demobbed, Brown found himself as a man in demand. His wartime exploits had drawn attention from English clubs and, after a brief return to Queen's Park, during which time he won his first Scotland cap, Brown had a big decision to make. Up to that point he had been an amateur player with the Spiders but had reached a crossroads at which all signposts pointed to a road into the professional game.

Falkirk were keen on giving him his professional break and so too were Manchester United, managed by Matt Busby. The rookie Old Trafford boss had played alongside Brown for

Scotland in 1945 in a match against the Auld Enemy in Birmingham, a game in which the goalkeeper's 'astonishing saves' drew lavish praise from the watching press corps.

The offer to join United was tempting but it was the lure of Ibrox that proved too strong for Brown to resist. He rebuffed Busby's approach and negotiated a bumper deal to join the Gers as the replacement for the retired Jerry Dawson, ensuring his talents were well rewarded. It also gave him the perfect start as he set off on a long and illustrious association with Rangers that brought honour after honour for the agile shot-stopper.

He became the founding member of the famed 'Iron Curtain' defence, the man who inspired the other great characters in that unique group and gave them the confidence to play to their potential. In his youth he had captained the West of Scotland schools select side and his leadership credentials, enhanced by the discipline and structure of navy life, came to the fore as he settled into life as a Rangers player in the booming post-war years of the Scottish game.

From the moment he signed at Ibrox he became central to everything the club achieved in that most fruitful of periods. He won three league championships, the Scottish Cup three times and the League Cup twice during a decade of glittering service.

The treble-winning season of 1948/49, when the Iron Curtain was at its strongest, was Brown's crowning glory. He played in every single minute of every single game as Rangers swept the board. The keeper was the only ever-present in that momentous season, the first time the club had ever won a treble, and his impressive displays between the sticks made him a huge favourite with the Ibrox crowd.

It was in fact the first time any team had won all of Scotland's domestic prizes in the same season and Brown's forty-four appearances ensured he was able to savour the achievement in its entirety. Dundee were beaten in the championship race by a point, Clyde were blown away 4-1 in the Scottish Cup and in the League Cup another shut-out helped Brown and his side to a 2-0 victory over Raith. It confirmed the club's total superiority that term.

Throughout his time with the club he remained a part-time player, reluctant to give up his position as a physical education teacher at Denny High School. Bill Struth attempted to change Brown's mind but he declined the request to give up his day job.

It did not do any harm to his form, with Brown proving to be the model of consistency. From August 1946 to April 1952 he played in every single one of Rangers' league matches, racking up 179 consecutive First Division outings, and in his 296 games for the team he kept 109 clean sheets. His statistics stand up to the closest scrutiny and Brown set the benchmark for all Rangers goalkeepers.

He represented the Scottish football League eight times and also won six Scotland caps, tasting defeat just once in those internationals. His debut came in 1946 against Belgium and he went on to feature against England, Wales, Switzerland and Northern Ireland, twice, up to his final match for the national side in 1952. His first appearance came while he was still registered with Queen's Park, giving Brown the distinction of being the last amateur ever to be capped by Scotland.

In the end it was the keeper's high standards and, ultimately, honesty that led to the curtain beginning to fall on Brown's career with the Light Blues. He shouldered the burden of responsibility for a 5-0 defeat against Hearts in the season opener of 1952 and, after admitting culpability, lost his first team place to George Niven.

It ended Brown's tenure as undisputed goalkeeping king at Ibrox after one of the very few dark points in a Rangers career full of impressive highlights. While it was not the final act for the great man as a Gers star, it began the ball rolling for his eventual exit.

After being dropped by Rangers in the wake of that 1952 League Cup defeat at Hearts, Brown persevered with the club for four years. He dotted in and out of the team as back-up to Niven for several seasons, but was given a way out by Falkirk, joining the Brockville side in 1956 as a thirty-something veteran. He was an instant hit with the Bairns but after an injury-disrupted second campaign he found himself out of the starting eleven and on the transfer list.

As he had done so often in his life up to that point, Brown spotted an opportunity to further his career and significantly expand his horizons. What happened next would set him on the path to one of the most significant periods in his life in sport.

With his playing days drawing to a close it was St Johnstone who stepped in to tap into the former Scotland cap's coaching credentials, offering him the chance to put them to good use as manager of their team.

He developed into a natural manager and born communicator, experiencing the best of both worlds by juggling his commitments with the Perth side and those associated with his role as a full-time teacher.

During nine enjoyable years with the Saints he won promotion to the First Division in 1960, the first time St Johnstone had occupied a seat at Scotland's top table in twenty-one years. Seven years later his stock as a coach reached its peak as Brown successfully won the race to become Scotland's next manager after the departure of John Prentice.

Kilmarnock's boss, Malcolm Macdonald had been in temporary charge of the national side and Brown's appointment came as a surprise to many, if not to those within the game who were aware of the regard in which he was held as a coach who first studied for his qualifications while still on the Rangers staff.

Brown had been headhunted by both Dundee United and Hibs during his St Johnstone tenure but rejected both approaches. He got his reward when the SFA committee men rubber-stamped his application for the country's top football job.

His first act was to guide his new charges to a famous 3-2 victory over World Cup winners England at Wembley just weeks after his appointment, but it was a rare highlight. Brown served four years in the role, dismissed in the summer of 1971 after failing to qualify for the 1972 European Championships. His record of nine wins in twenty-seven internationals was not helped by internal problems, with issues surrounding the SFA selection committee and continued problems with the availability of Scotland stars based in England. After thirteen years managing club and country, Brown called time on his coaching career to concentrate on interests outside of the game.

Just as Brown's natural ability as a coach and tutor had been spotted during his Royal Navy days, so too were the identical qualities quickly identified in Rangers' colleague Billy Williamson after he had joined the same force. Despite his status as a football star, it was teaching that became Williamson's vocation for the bulk of his life and he had a natural aptitude for leading teams. In civilian life those skills were put to good use in a long and fondly remembered school career, but as a serviceman he was pressed into action as a physical training instructor in the disciplined world of the navy.

He was a wet-behind-the-ears student, learning his trade at Jordanhill College, when the war broke out in 1939. At the start of the 1930s the college had been nominated as the one and only institution for the training of male physical education teachers in Scotland, ensuring a string of prominent Former Pupils to its credit among the nation's rugby and football fraternity. Those undertaking teacher training were excused service in the armed forces along with select other occupations, although for

Williamson it was only a matter of time before he was free of those commitments and joined the line of volunteers.

He was naturally assigned to training duties and joined the swelling ranks of navy fitness experts. Following the First World War there was a concerted effort to add more physical training instructors, with an emphasis not only on the hard graft meted out to new recruits but also for more general exercise and recreational pursuits for more mature members of the service.

The so called 'Swedish System' had been adopted by the armed forces early in the twentieth century, following a programme focussing very much on discipline, strength, balance and agility. Long before aerobics, the navy top brass had recognised the importance of working on heart and lungs to ensure a fighting fit group was ready to meet the challenge of war, and the P.T. instructors were entrusted with following the mantra and taking it to the masses. Of course, it helped that so many were able to lead by example and clearly practised what they preached to enable them to play football at the highest level. Williamson was still a young man when he served, yet he already had an impressive track record in sport to point to as he set about imposing himself. He was also a powerful figure physically, a factor that must have been a major advantage in the highly charged atmosphere of the forces.

The Glaswegian, a sporting all-rounder in his youth while growing up and a keen rugby player during his school days at Lenzie Academy, first showed promise as a junior player with Kirkintilloch Rob Roy.

He combined those playing commitments with his teacher training and moved on to Petershill in the junior ranks before being spotted by Rangers and recruited in 1941 during the wartime competition.

He was an instant hit at Ibrox, scoring on his debut in a league win at home to Airdrie, but put the brakes on his Gers career to join the navy. While serving in England he was able to keep his football instincts sharp by turning out for Manchester City as a very welcome guest. The bullish Williamson, in both physique and never-say-die attitude, was a valuable addition to any team.

The appearances for City added to the experience he had gained in his early appearances for Rangers and he continued to feature at Ibrox through the war years on a sporadic basis. One of his outings was in the famous challenge match against Dynamo Moscow when the Russian tourists touched down in the closing weeks of 1945, with Glasgow still in the grip of post-war austerity. A glamour friendly against the impressive Dynamo was just what the doctor ordered, something to whet the appetite and put a bounce back in the stride of the Gers faithful.

Williamson, still a young man at just twenty-two when the Muscovites arrived, was ready to take centre stage. His powerful forward runs won two penalties in a pulsating encounter, with one of those converted by George Young on the way to a 2-2 draw against the visitors.

For the Russians it was part of a trip into the western world to attempt to prove their superiority – with wins over Arsenal and Cardiff, as well as a draw against Chelsea, no doubt pleasing the leaders back home as they awaited news of every fixture.

For Rangers it was a workout in preparation for their return to competitive football.

When normal service resumed in the 1946/47 season it was the Light Blues who sat atop the Scottish pile at the end of the campaign – and Williamson had played a significant part in that. He scored vital goals in that title-winning run, including four against Clyde in a 5-0 trouncing of the Bully Wee and two at home to Hamilton Accies on the last afternoon of a memorable term as Rangers won 4-1. Struth's side had clinched the coveted prize with a two-point lead over closest challengers Hibs.

The lad from Lenzie had won his first honour with the club earlier in the season when he scored in a 4-0 victory over Aberdeen in the first ever League Cup final.

The striker was rated highly by the Ibrox manager, who handed him the prized Number 9 shirt for the start of the 1947/48 season, as a player and as a man. Indeed, it was Williamson that Struth requested a visit from in the days before his death. But with a galaxy of attacking stars on the books, it was in a support role that Williamson was to shine in the years ahead.

During the 1947/48 campaign he had been a bystander as his team mates marched to the final of the Scottish Cup. He was in the stands again as Rangers drew 1-1 against Morton in the final. For the replay there was a lifeline – Williamson was in from the cold. The match attracted what was a record midweek crowd of close to 134,000 and the sailor rose to the big occasion. His header, five minutes from the end of extra-time, was the only goal of a tense replay and the late call-up proved to be the match-winning hero.

The forward also won a recall for the 1949 Scottish Cup final and repaid Bill Struth with a goal in the 4-1 win over Clyde, before adding to his collection of honours when he starred in the 1949/50 First Division championship success, contributing eleven goals in nineteen appearances.

Despite Williamson's success, both individually with his impressive rate of goals to appearances as well as in team honours while he was in the line-up, there was no long-term future for him at Ibrox. He had been adept at working as an able deputy – but fierce competition for places ensured he had to accept the frustrating role of understudy, or look for regular first team football elsewhere. He took the difficult decision to go for the latter and seek fresh pastures.

He switched to St Mirren early in 1951 and moved on to

Stirling Albion a year later for a three-season spell, bringing an end to a playing career that had seen him impress at the highest level. But it was not necessarily on the park that Williamson excelled the most, as his 'second' career would testify to.

He went on to spend forty years on the staff at Lenzie Academy as a physical education teacher and also assistant rector, where he truly found his forte as a man who to this day remains fondly remembered by those who studied under him.

Rugby, a sport he returned to play after his time in senior football drew to a close, was a major passion for Williamson and he is credited with laying the foundations for the town's successful team by fostering the oval ball game at the academy with familiar passion and attention to detail.

In fairness, he had also demonstrated an aptitude for developing young football talent and had a spell as coach of Queen's Park in the 1950s. Among the young prospects to fall under the wing of the wily trainer at Hampden during that spell was a certain Alex Ferguson, who is said to have thrived during his brief tutelage by a past-master.

The dalliance with coaching in the Scottish Football League did not extend beyond his time with the Spiders. School life took over from that point and he became immersed with sport at a more raw level. A man whose football ability shone so bright and won him an opportunity at the highest level is remembered as a teacher who treated every pupil with the same care and attention, whether a budding star or youngster struggling with the basics. Effort, not brilliance, is what Mr Williamson is said to have placed above all else.

He devoted his professional life to the academy and its pupils, while also finding the time to get involved nationally with schools rugby and athletics, as well as indulging his own passion for curling and golf.

Williamson, who died in 2006 at the age of eighty-three,

played not only alongside Bobby Brown in the Royal Navy old boys' network during his Rangers days. There was another Second World War veteran of the seas in the team of the late 1940s, with Jimmy Parlane the man in question.

The striker was never a regular at Ibrox but had a knack of scoring important goals at important times when he was given a chance in the first team. He had first been discovered during the war years and was part of the championship-winning side when the First Division resumed in 1946/47.

His first competitive goal was an Old Firm clincher at Celtic Park early in that victorious season and he scored his second of the campaign, in only his fourth appearance, on the final day of the season.

In the face of stiff competition from Willie Thornton and Jimmy Duncanson, among others, Parlane made just a single appearance the following term and went on to play for Airdrie. The Rangers FP, who ran a market garden business in the Argyll village of Rhu, saw his connection to Ibrox rekindled when his son Derek burst onto the scene in the early 1970s and rose to become a goalscoring Gers hero.

12

THE PROUD HIGHLANDER

The Second World War was remembered in different ways by different servicemen across the globe. For some, the medals and decorations of the battles of 1939 to 1945 provide a tangible nod to that period in time. For others the images locked away in the memory bank are the hidden reminders of their experiences in the forces. For one man the era was evident every day as he watched his young family grow and blossom in the post-war years, in a world freed of tyranny and brutality of the regime his peers fought with pride and purpose to overcome.

Sammy Cox was a teenager when war was declared. A young man setting out on what, even at a tender age, appeared a glittering future as the football world began to sit up and take note of the small but powerful defender with pace, poise and instinctive ability. The events that followed simply delayed rather than curtailed his seemingly inevitable sporting stardom, and the lessons in discipline and fighting spirit imparted during his years of service in the army were carried forward to give an added spur to his pursuit of excellence.

The Ayrshire lad entered the service as a boy and emerged a man who had shouldered responsibility for helping to train the nation's fighting force as a physical training instructor with the renowned Gordon Highlanders. He left his familiar home turf on the west coast to up sticks and join the Gordons in Aberdeen, as raw recruits and experienced soldiers were whipped into shape for the rigours awaiting them on the continent. The time he spent with that famous regiment made a lasting impression on Cox who never forgot the part they played in shaping his future. But then, how could he?

Jean Cox, who took on the famous surname when she married her football playing fiancé in 1949, takes up the story. She explained:

Sammy enjoyed his time in Aberdeen with the Gordon High-landers immensely. He spent a couple of years serving in the army and the experience stood him in good stead for the rest of his life.

His colonel with the Gordon Highlanders, Colonel McGregor, was a great sportsman and encouraged Sammy to keep playing throughout the war. He would give him leave at weekends to play in fixtures and give him the opportunity to travel back home to Ayrshire to see his family. When we came to naming our third son we were looking for inspiration, and I suggested Gordon McGregor Cox – Gordon after the Gordon Highlanders and McGregor after his colonel in the army. Sammy liked that idea and that's what we decided upon.

Sammy Cox is one of the few surviving Rangers men from the war years. Now past his eighty-seventh birthday, the Ibrox legend is lovingly cared for by his wife and staff at the nursing home where he lives in the Canadian city of Stratford. The family emigrated to North America in the 1950s and have remained there ever since. Cox, a household name in the Scottish game, is held in the same regard in his adopted home-land. Stratford, in the state of Ontario, may be better known for its ice hockey players who have played NHL more than for its football prowess, but in Cox the city boasts a famous resident with an impressive sporting pedigree.

Despite his long absence from Scottish soil, Cox has never let go of his roots or been allowed to forget his achievements in the light blue of his beloved Rangers. In 2001 he was awarded honorary life membership of the North American Rangers Supporters Association, having lent his assistance to the group over a number of years.

Cox and his wife were guests of honour of NARSA on a number of occasions and were paid visits by the likes of Alex McLeish and Willie Henderson at different intervals. Those gestures meant much to a man who had taken pride in his Rangers connection, and in Canada as much as in Scotland he is remembered first and foremost as a loyal light blue servant. Indeed, the contribution of Cox has been noted in glorious technicolour in the form of a giant banner depicting a portrait of the star man flanked by the American and Canadian flags unfurled at Ibrox.

It was under the British flag that he was enlisted to the army in the early 1940s. His athletic abilities earned him a place on the P.T. staff, serving at the Granite City's barracks and putting the troops through their paces on a daily basis. He was not the only footballer to serve with the Gordon Highlanders, with Celtic's C.S.M. Cook among the ranks of P.T. instructors. Preparation was key to the battle plans and stamina vital for the soldiers awaiting deployment. There was only a short time with which to work with the troops and the instructors needed to quickly gain the respect of the men falling under their wing. It was a daunting assignment for any young rookie, but there was little time to waste as the war effort intensified.

The regiment had been involved from the outset, facing stern challenges at every turn. Two battalions of the Gordons sur-rendered at St Valery in 1940 as Britain's list of casualties grew, although those two units regrouped and went on to play a successful part in the battles of North Africa and Sicily. On D-Day in 1944 they, and an additional Gordon Highlanders battalion, were part of the push through France, Belgium and the Nerthlands on the way to victory against the enemy. The Highlanders also saw action in Singapore and Burma, with these commitments ensuring a steady stream of men were put through their paces back at base to ready them for action.

While the physical training instructors were heavily occupied with their duties at base in Scotland, Cox did make excursions to the battle-hit regions of Europe during his time in the forces. The trips were not without their dramas as the perils of travel during that period were highlighted more than once.

Jean Cox said:

Although he was never out of Aberdeen with the Gordons, Sammy did travel during the war to play matches overseas. On one occasion they were forced to turn back because there were German planes near to their own aircraft.

It was also through the army that Sammy ended up playing for Dundee in the wartime games as Colonel McGregor was great friends with the Dundee manager and an agreement was reached.

George Anderson was the Dens manager in question, also serving on the board at Dundee before taking the helm officially when peace was restored and competitive football resumed in 1946. The Englishman is credited with turning the Dark Blues into a major force in the Scottish game, having taken charge when the club were confined to the second tier of the domestic game. During the wartime games he was able to call on the considerable talents of Cox, who had also turned out for Queen's Park and Third Lanark closer to home.

While those club games provided the youngster with a good grounding in the senior game, it was a match for the British Army football team that provided the international in the making with his steepest learning curve. Typically for a man renowned for his professionalism, he took the lesson in his stride.

The fixture in question was played in Aberdeen and Cox was part of an army outfit that tackled their RAF counterparts in front of an enthusiastic north-east crowd, gathered in the shadow of Pittodrie for the intriguing encounter.

Cox, still a teenager, was not the man in the spotlight. Instead the full glare of the public and media was directed at Sir Stanley Matthews in airforce colours. Up against the wing wonder that day was Cox, who proved adept in either full back berth and as a wing half during his career.

Jean Cox recalls:

The RAF were favourites to win with Stanley Matthews in their side, with all his tricks. It was the first time Sammy had been up against Matthews but it did not faze him. When he was later chosen to play for Scotland in an international against England, much was made of the presence of Stanley Matthews in the team and the fact Sammy would be up against him. Very few people realised he had played against him in that army match and everyone was saying 'he'll take you to the cleaners' and all the rest. In fact it was quite the opposite; after the match the head-lines said 'Cox held Matthews' and he never once got the better of Sammy. That one match Sammy had played against him up in Aberdeen had given him all the confidence he needed

We all travelled down to London that day, myself and Sammy's dad and mother. I couldn't watch for the first half hour because I was so nervous – but I shouldn't have been. Sammy had no qualms about playing against Matthews going into the match, mainly because of that match up in Aberdeen that he had played previously, and just as he had said, there was no need for him to be troubled. He was never worried at all and played that way.

That Auld Enemy showdown took place in the spring of 1949, when the visiting Scots humbled their Wembley hosts in a 3-1 win courtesy of goals from Jimmy Mason, Billy Steel and Lawrie Reilly. It was one of twenty-five appearances that Cox, by then ensconced in the Rangers team, made in the dark blue of his country. His debut came in Paris in 1948 against the French, and his final cap was won against England six years later at Hampden, when Cox was awarded the honour of the captaincy to mark the occasion.

It was his displays as part of the famous Iron Curtain defence at Ibrox that won Cox his place on the international stage. The famous back line of the 1940s and '50s was marshalled by Royal Navy pilot Bobby Brown. Not surprisingly, Brown was not the only forces trained player in a formidable back line that set about its football task with military precision.

When Cox was demobbed from the army he was able to begin life as a professional footballer, signing for Rangers in April 1946 to make his light blue dream a reality. What followed was an impeccable career at Ibrox which brought Cox admirers from far and wide, as well as a treasure trove of medals from a glorious period for the club.

He was left-footed but just as comfortable on the right, and his stylish approach to defending saw Cox likened to a South American by some observers, although his vigorous tackling and toughness were unmistakably Scottish. His combined abilities won Cox a place in the Rangers Hall of Fame and he travelled to Scotland in 2003 to accept his place among the pantheon of Ibrox superstars whose names will forever be part of the fabric of the club. The name of Sammy Cox sits comfortably on that list of immortals.

The Darvel-born player clocked up more than three hundred appearances in nine years at Ibrox, rarely putting a foot wrong and missing only a handful of games along the way. The championship was won in his first season at Ibrox and Cox, with thirteen appearances in the league that term, had a part to play.

By the time he won the Scottish Cup in 1948 the defender was established as a permanent fixture in the side, and he missed just a single match of the forty-four played in the treble-winning season of 1948/49. That campaign was a defining one for the Brown, Young, Shaw, McColl, Woodburn and Cox defence. They conceded thirty-two goals in thirty league games – a defensive record sixteen goals better than runners-up Dundee who were just one point behind when the finishing line was crossed. That stubbornness in defence proved to be the difference between success and failure in the title race, just as it did the following season when the title flag fluttered over the famous old ground once again when Hibs were pipped by a single point. This time the renowned back division leaked just twenty-six goals, growing as individuals and as a unit. Cox and his team mates won the Scottish Cup in 1950 to cap another fine year. In 1953 he featured in his fourth First Division winning side, when Hibs lost out on goal difference in a fiercely contested fight for the honour, and the Cox medal collection was complete.

He had lived the dream, not only playing with the Rangers badge on his chest but doing so during an era in which the club was enjoying considerable success against some very accomplished opposition sides.

Those achievements did not go unnoticed among the international selectors and Cox went on to have a long and impressive Scotland career. When he made his debut against France, in a 3-0 defeat, he did so in bizarre circumstances. The Rangers man was drafted into the team just minutes before kick-off when Morton player Billy Campbell's toecap broke off his boot in the warm up, and prevented him from playing – but there was nothing fortunate about his performances in dark blue thereafter. It was all down to his outstanding ability.

Cox became a Scotland stalwart and first served as skipper during a tour of America, prior to captaining the side against the Auld Enemy in 1954. It was a fitting honour for a national treasure who never let his country down, on or off the park. Having had to contend with barbed wire, mud, water and simulated fire during his army training, he always stood firm in the face of pressure both as a soldier and during his playing days.

Cox, renowned for his outstanding balance and cool nature, had started out on the road to stardom with Loudon Star juveniles in his native Ayrshire before graduating to represent Darvel in the junior ranks. He was still only seventeen when Queen's Park offered a route into the senior game, and it was a chance Cox grabbed with both hands. The defender progressed up the football ladder with Third Lanark but when war broke out football took a back seat.

During the conflict he represented Dundee but it was Rangers who nipped in when peace was restored in time for the 1946/47 season to sign one of the game's hottest properties to the club he was so desperate to represent. The defender shared his manager Bill Struth's devotion to the cause, and he eventually became a father figure at Ibrox as he guided the next generation through their fledgling days on the staff, always willing to lend an ear and to pass on his considerable experience. A man who had seen it all and done it all was well placed to pass on advice.

Cox was eventually released by Rangers in the summer of 1956 and, despite being two years past his thirtieth birthday, was quickly snapped up by former Rangers goalkeeper Jerry Dawson, who by that stage was in charge of East Fife. Despite his advancing years, Cox was still a formidable physical force, and there was talk of a Scotland recall once he had blown away the cobwebs with the Bayview side.

The additional cap never did materialise but Cox did get a second wind in career terms. In 1958 he moved to Canada to take on a player-coach role with Ulster United in Toronto.

Toronto Ulster United, founded in 1914, have gone down in the nation's soccer folklore as one of the leading clubs in the history of the domestic game in Canada. They had been post-war league winners in 1946 and 1951 and Cox was brought in at a time when they were determined to regain their place at the top of the tree.

Ulster United clearly saw the benefit of bringing in a high-profile recruit from Ibrox. They had twice played host to Rangers in friendly matches in the 1920s and '30s, and there had been a long-standing affection for all things Scottish and Rangers among the support. The tour match in 1930 attracted a crowd of 9,000 eager fans, the type of attendance that Canadian teams had previously only dreamt of.

Prior to the more modern creation of the all-encompassing North American Soccer League, Canada boasted its own thriving national championship with feeder district leagues, and Toronto Ulster United were part of that scene when Cox arrived on foreign shores to begin his long association with the country. He was no stranger though, having been part of the Scotland squad that successfully toured Canada in 1949 and left unbeaten after nine matches against local sides, select teams and, to round off the trip, a 4-0 trouncing of the USA national side.

Toronto Ultser United eventually disbanded in 1963, by which time Cox had long since moved on. He spent a season with United before joining fledgling city rivals Toronto Sparta – one of a number of clubs that had sprung up in the 1950s in a soccer scene buoyed by the influx of new citizens from throughout western and eastern Europe.

It was a vital injection of fresh blood after the Second World War had left football struggling to find its feet after the enforced hibernation caused by the service in Europe of the country's armed forces.

The 1950s sparked the game back into life, with wonderfully named teams such as the Toronto Ukrainians, Toronto East End Canadians, the White Eagles, the Toronto Hungarians, Toronto Italia and Toronto Hakoah pointing towards the multiculturalism gripping the sporting scene in the city. Toronto Sparta had entered the fold in 1955.

Cox spent a year in their colours before moving away from the big city and settling in Stratford, recruited by the local team to guide them on and off the park. He also won selection for the Ontario All-Stars state team along the way.

The family had settled well in the area and found a home from home. Jean Cox added:

Our wedding was in 1949 and we have spent the majority of our married life in Canada. Sammy had an uncle out here and it was he who suggested we should move with our three sons. Although Sammy was reluctant to leave Scotland behind at first, we have never regretted the decision. All these years later we are still in Canada and have a wonderful quality of life for the family.

You can take the girl out of Scotland, but never Scotland out of the girl. The familiar tartan tint to the accent of Jean Cox, well over half a century since she and her husband bid farewell to their homeland, hints that the family's roots have never been forgotten and certainly not disguised by these proud Scots.

She said:

He enjoyed the responsibility he had as a P.T. instructor in the army and he went on to coach in football when we came to Canada, when the Toronto team asked him to come out. We have never looked back. I'm eighty-six now and have enjoyed a great life here in Canada.

In time we were invited down to Stratford to help out the football team and were very well looked after by the club. Of course they call it soccer here – but I hate that word. It will always be football to me. We headed down, with all three children in a little Volkswagen, and have been here ever since. It's a wonderful city, with a country feel. Sammy is now being looked after in a nursing home just up the hill from our house.

Cox is now nearing his ninetieth birthday but has lost none of the determination that made him such a hero in his homeland, insisting on walking unaided in a nod to the fitness that was such an integral part of his stardom. Until recently the couple were familiar figures at Rangers supporters' functions.

Jean Cox added:

We used to go to all of the NARSA conventions and have always been invited. The last one was just two or three weeks ago in Florida and I would loved to have gone to that one, although I know it is Sammy that everyone would want to see. It just wasn't possible for us to attend.

I've got pictures in front of me of Willie Waddell, Willie Thornton, so many other great players from that famous Rangers team that Sammy played in. Sadly most have now passed away. I hope the memories stay alive because they were a great unit and a fantastic team.

13

LIGHT AMID THE GLOOM

Rangers 8, Celtic 1. To this day that Old Firm score remains the record margin of victory in the world's most famous derby game and it is an achievement that will surely never be beaten. Or will it? The team that ran out at Ibrox on New Year's day in 1943 to tackle Celtic could not have imagined the way in which they would systematically dismantle their fierce city rivals, yet they did it in style. With belief, class and a touch of fortune it is true to say that anything is possible. Records are, after all, there to be broken.

The fact that famous result fell during a wartime league fixture mattered not a jot to the Rangers support in the crowd of 30,000 for that winter's afternoon extravaganza. It was a performance to warm the hearts at a time when the protracted war against the Germans was a huge cause of concern for everyone in the country.

The team that lined up that day was: Dawson, Gray, Shaw, Little, Young, Symon, Waddell, Duncanson, Gillick, Venters and Johnston. On paper it looked like a formidable side and on grass it proved to be just that.

The irrepressible character of Torrance Gillick was the man who led the charge, bagging a hat-trick in the rout as team mates

Willie Waddell and George Young each grabbed a double. Jimmy Duncanson was the other goalscorer.

The treble from Gillick was a sweet moment for the Ibrox crowd as they once again cheered a man who had been a hero to them before being lured away to the free-spending world of the English game.

Gillick, who was a winger with junior side Petershill when first spotted, was snapped up by Bill Struth in 1933, and in time played in every one of the forward positions for the club. He tasted success in the 1935 Scottish Cup final, part of the team which defeated Hamilton 2-1 to lift the trophy, and added a league championship winner's medal in the same season, but was the subject of a club record £8,000 bid by Everton later that year and made the move to Merseyside. Gillick had just turned twenty but the Airdrie-born starlet was a highly coveted prospect.

The lively character was not daunted by his new surroundings and proved a hit in England, with his form helping him to win all five of his Scotland caps while on the Goodison Park books. He scored three goals for the national team and never finished on the losing side.

It was during the war years that Gillick was able to return to Rangers while on leave from his service in the army and once again proved to be a hit with the Gers fans. The old adage about never returning to a club was well and truly blasted out of the water with his star showing in the Old Firm trouncing of Celtic.

If Struth's mind had not already been made up, that performance must have helped persuade the manager that Gillick should be given a second chance when normal service resumed following the war.

He was no longer a young man making his way in the game, but he displayed the same appetite for the game when the First Division burst back into life in 1946/47, a key man in the championship victory that season and on the score sheet in the 4-0 win over Aberdeen in the League Cup final.

He proved to be a man for the big occasion – the larger the crowd, the more determined Gillick was to make an impact. In the Scottish Cup final of 1948 he was the scorer as Rangers were held to a 1-1 draw against Morton in front of close to 132,000 fans at Hampden, and part of the team that finished the job four days later with a 1-0 win in the replay, when nearly 134,000 were crammed into the national stadium.

In 1948/49 he added to his collection of cup final goals when his strike helped put Raith Rovers to the sword in the League Cup showpiece, opening the Rangers' account as they edged to a 2-0 win.

That proved to be the Lanarkshire man's swansong with the club he had served on both sides of the war. He moved on to Partick Thistle and spent two years with the Jags before retiring at the age of thirty-seven. Gillick's contribution to the Rangers cause has been recognised with his addition to the hall of fame.

Gillick and his team mates Adam Little, Willie Waddell and George Young would, in time, be able to sympathise with Celtic's playing staff. Ten months after rattling eight past the Hoops, all four men were part of the Scotland team that was picked apart by England on their way to an 8-0 defeat against their Auld Enemy adversaries at Maine Road in Manchester. Everton's Tommy Lawton was unplayable that day, scoring four goals.

For the duration of the Second World War the Auld Enemy set their differences aside to unite under the British flag. The Scots and English fought side by side on all fronts in the Allied effort and formed a force that struck fear into the hearts of the enemy. That unity was a cornerstone of the victory and re-mained intact for almost the entire duration of the war. The exception was when a size five piece of leather was placed between the two proud factions. On those occasions, the national divide sprung up once more to bring a slice of normality to the most irregular of times.

The wartime internationals became part and parcel of the restricted football calendar and the clashes between Scotland and England, even in those times of austerity, had the ability to pull supporters out in their droves. Scotland had their successes, with a 3-2 win in Newcastle against the English in 1941, but nothing as impressive as the eight-goal salvo in Manchester.

For one man in the team that day the reason was simple:

That afternoon at Maine Road, on paper, we had a great Scots team. Tommy Walker and Tory Gillick were great international inside forwards for Scotland. Willie Waddell was a powerful right winger. George Young and Jimmy Carabine were great players. It was simply that Stan Cullis's England team was among the all-time greats.

That was the assessment of Dr Adam Little, who featured at inside left for Scotland as he had done for Rangers in the 8-1 victory against Celtic earlier in the year. They were two extremes of a career in football that served the good doctor well.

The boy from Blantyre, a Rutherglen Academy FP, blossomed into an international player of great repute after being plucked from school football by Rangers and Bill Struth. He was farmed out to Blantyre Victoria to toughen up for the challenges ahead and he had an early taste of success when he was promoted to the Rangers team in 1940, in time for the Scottish Emergency War Cup final win against Dundee United at Hampden.

He continued to progress until leaving Glasgow behind in 1943 to join the Royal Army Medical Corps, with whom he travelled the world as a military medic after initially finding himself stationed south of the border.

While gearing up for the rigours of war, Little discovered that there was more to army life than the cold hard realities of battle.

Prior to his death in 2008, Little penned some memories of his service days, and those notes are now part of the collection at the McLean Museum in Greenock. Little recalled:

I was called up to the army on a Saturday, and on that Saturday we were playing Celtic, so I wrote to the CO and asked if I could be excused. He let me off. The sergeant in the mess was a fellow I played football with, a goalkeeper with Blantyre Vics. This fellow Gillespie said there's a doctor in Aldershot who wants to see you, Jimmy McKillop. He wants you to go up for afternoon tea. I go away along to Aldershot and there's tea-dancing and so there's my introduction to the army.

While I was there I played for the Arsenal. I'd leave on the Friday, go up and stay in a hotel in London, Arsenal paid my digs. The boys used to come up on the Saturday and they stayed in the hotel room. They couldn't get accommodation so they slept on the floor, three or four of my pals.

When I went out to the Middle East, I arrived at the transit camp. The CO posted me to GHQ Cairo Surplus T as a surplus doctor – I was posted there so I could play football for the army. I played for the army and the combined team, the Wanderers against the Egyptians and the CO says to me: 'Well we've got to beat these Egyptians.' I said there's only one way, to select fourteen, fifteen players and all stay together and train together. We did that for a fortnight. The boys were all excused duties and we played them and won. The CO said what would you like to do now and I said: 'I'd like to do a tour of Cyprus.' Right! It was organised, we went to Cyprus. A cook's tour!

The soldiers came from miles around. The Wanderers had International players – like Harry Johnstone, Andy McLaren. We went all over Palestine and it was amazing, the fellows were fed up with life really, confined to barracks, and areas and the like. They appreciated the football teams coming to play for them.

Opportunities for Little at Rangers were restricted in the post-war years and he was picked up by Morton in 1951, enjoying a four-year spell and establishing himself as a Cappielow favourite. After hanging up his boots Little concentrated on his medical career as a GP in Port Glasgow, where he remained until his retirement from the profession.

While he had been a fringe man at Ibrox, many of his fellow army men went on to carve out long and successful careers in the first team during the hugely successful period after the war.

It was the emergence of the Iron Curtain unit that cost Davie Gray his place in the Rangers side. After serving with the army in the Middle East during the war, he started the 1946/47 season as first choice right back but, as the team galloped towards the title, he was edged out by George Young after the inspirational captain's move out of the centre of the defence. Gray played nine times in that league-winning campaign and in three League Cup ties before joining Preston North End in the summer of 1947.

The Dundonian, who played junior football with Lochee Harp, was twenty-four when he made his first appearance for the Gers but played his best years in England. After a year with Preston, where he was an automatic pick, he moved to Blackburn Rovers and held down the right back role at Ewood Park for four seasons.

As Gray was leaving, a young man by the name of Willie Paton was ready to establish himself on the big stage for Rangers. Paton scored the second goal of the game as Raith Rovers were beaten 2-0 in the League Cup final of 1948/49 to prove he had the right temperament to be a Ranger.

It was Paton's first contribution to the League Cup bid but he had a more extensive involvement in the other strands of the treble adventure that season. Although he sat out the Scottish Cup final through injury he had played in all four of the ties leading to it. He was also made nineteen league appearances en route to the championship flag.

The former Kirkintilloch Rob Roy attacker played in more than 150 games for the club, completing his full set of domestic prizes when he played in the 1953 Scottish Cup final against Aberdeen, before leaving in 1956 to join Ayr United.

He had been sent on the road to stardom by Kirkintilloch during the war years, winning the Scottish Junior Cup in 1943 as football dovetailed with national service, and within four years earned his big move to Rangers. Willie Paton died in 2005.

Dave Marshall was another one of the talents introduced on the back of army service. He scored three goals in his first three games for the club, scoring on his debut in a 3-0 win at home to Airdrie in November 1947 and followed that performance up with goals against Queen of the South at Palmerston in another 3-0 win and again in a 2-1 triumph at Clyde. Marshall, an inside forward with an eye for goal, drew a blank in his fourth match against Morton and lost his place to Jimmy Duncanson as a result. Marshall continued to be a regular scorer during his sporadic recalls to the first team, playing his last match in 1952.

At the other end of the spectrum was Archie Macaulay, who was already an experienced professional by the time Britain went to war in 1939. With that expertise behind him, Macaulay was put to work as a physical training instructor with the army.

The Falkirk-born player had been introduced to the Rangers team by Bill Struth in the 1933/34 season, a championship-winning campaign in which the wing half played a small but nonetheless important part. He made his debut in a 2-0 win at Ayr and played in four further games that term, scoring a vital goal in a 2-1 win at Hamilton as the term neared its conclusion.

He was just eighteen when he made his first appearance in the top team and was already proving he had what it took to play in the man's game. In his second season he featured in sixteen of the thirty-eight First Division matches as Struth's team charged to another title triumph, and the youngster also had a part to play in the 1936/37 championship win when he appeared nine times.

Like so many players of his generation, Macaulay was still a young man when war broke out. His period of service proved to be a line in the sand as far as football was concerned, with the post-war years providing a whole new chapter as the Scot took his talents to an English audience.

London became home for the industrious midfielder as he embarked on a productive run with a succession of capital clubs, starting at West Ham and then moving on to Brentford and Arsenal in quick succession. He settled at Highbury at the start of the 1947/48 season, and over the course of three years with the Gunners he made more than a century of appearances. As his thirty-fifth birthday loomed, Macaulay moved to Fulham in 1950 and was a regular over the course of two campaigns with the Craven Cottage outfit. His career at the top level had stretched over twenty years and he served with distinction throughout.

John Galloway's time as a Ranger was only just beginning when football stalled for the war years. Born in Bo'ness in 1918, he first appeared on a team sheet early in 1938. He went on to make a handful of appearances the following season, in 1938/39, when Bill Struth's side won the league. Used as a wing half and inside forward, he made a clutch of appearances for Rangers in wartime football before trying his hand in the English game with Chelsea in the 1946/47 campaign. After finding opportunities limited at Stamford Bridge, the former Ibrox man moved on to Leyton.

It was a familiar story for many players who saw the war slice through their Rangers dream. For Ralph Cowan that was particularly true. On Saturday 26 August 1939, the world appeared to be opening up in front of Cowan as he ran out to deputise for Jock Shaw in the left back slot, and helped his team to a 3-1 win against Arbroath. The Red Lichties were no pushovers, holding their own in the scrap among the smaller teams to preserve top-flight status, but were no match for Rangers. Two wins and a draw up to that point had Struth's men on track for another championship and the rookie defender must have had high hopes that he would be in it for the long haul, even if there was the formidable figure of Shaw ahead of him in the pecking order.

Then, just five days later, the whole world was turned upside down. The declaration of war ensured there was just one further competitive game after Cowan's debut and, despite the occasional appearance during the war years, he was not part of the plans by the time the fighting ended.

In the wartime league in the 1939/40 season he filled in for Shaw, and also for Davie Gray on the right side of the defence, comfortable in either of the full back berths, but was in the right place at the wrong time as the opportunity was nipped in the bud before he had truly got into his stride as a fully fledged top-flight performer. His one competitive outing was followed by half a dozen during the war years, during which time he served in the army.

Chris McNee's two seasons with Rangers were wrapped around the war. He had joined the Ibrox cause in 1939 after starring for Hamilton Accies, with his performances on the left wing earning promotion to the Scottish League Select side prior to his switch to Rangers.

Accies were serious contenders during the 1930s. Although McNee was not part of the side that defeated the Gers in the 1935 Scottish Cup final, he was part of the Hamilton side during an era in which they consistently finished in the top half of the top flight.

When he joined Bill Struth at Rangers it was to step into a team that held the Scottish crown. The task facing him was helping his new club retain the title and he was viewed as a successor to Davie Kinnear, featuring in four of the five matches in the First Division before the league was halted in response to the outbreak of war. While he continued to turn out in the Scottish Regional League Western Division and played in every round of the Scottish Emergency War Cup up to the final against Dundee United, McNee was soon ruled out of the equation.

It was not until normal service resumed in 1946/47 that he returned to the Rangers fold and picked up where he left off, patrolling the left wing beat after being restored to the Number 11 jersey as winter fell. McNee went on to play ten games in the title-winning campaign and scored three goals along the way in wins against Clyde, Hamilton and Hearts. He joined Dumbarton the following year as his career wound down, the best years sapped by the demands of the war.

Former Govan High School pupil Eddie Rutherford had to be patient as he waited for his break with his local club. Having served his apprenticeship with Battlefield Amateurs and Mossvale YMCA, he was recruited by Bill Struth in 1941. It was not until the competitive action resumed in 1946/47 that Rutherford finally made his entrance, given his chance on the right wing and remaining in the squad until he switched to Hearts as part of the swap deal that took Colin Liddell to Ibrox.

He had signed for Gers as an impressionable teenager but was eventually blooded as a battle-hardened man. After his experiences overseas it was little surprise that the peculiar pressures of life as an Old Firm player did not faze him.

Rutherford was a true Rangers great and emerged from his time at Ibrox with a glittering array of medals to prove it. He starred on both the right flank and the left wing over the course of six years as a Gers player and was never happier than when turning opposition defences inside out.

He was pitched in as Willie Waddell's deputy on the right side of the park. It was an incredibly tough act to follow but Rutherford, by then in his mid-twenties, was up to the task and slotted in admirably as required. His appearances included five in the league winning side and another in the League Cup final trouncing of Aberdeen, when Waddell was forced to sit out the 4-0 victory over the Dons through injury.

Rutherford was part of the Scottish Cup winning team in 1947/48 and on the back of that success he was introduced to the international scene, making his one and only appearance for Scotland in a 3-0 defeat against France in Paris on the right wing.

Out-and-out wingers were integral to the style of football in the 1940s and '50s and Scotland had a proud history of producing flankers with natural ability and the type of energy and drive that became such a trademark of the national game. Rutherford had all of that and more, as he had to live in the exalted company of one of the finest squads ever assembled at Ibrox.

He was a star of the treble-winning line-up in the 1948/49 campaign, having switched to the left wing by then to enable Waddell to be twinned with him in the same side to devastating effect.

The historic triple crown, the first ever in Scottish football, was followed by a league and Scottish Cup double, and Rutherford remained an important part of Bill Struth's master plan until he began to wind down in the 1951/52 season. He had been a Ranger as man and boy, a committed servant and loyal club man.

Rutherford moved to Hearts in 1951. He also had spells with Raith Rovers and Hamilton Accies before retiring.

Stalwart Jimmy Simpson was a wonderful servant for club and country. He broke into the Rangers team in the late 1920s. He learned his trade under the legendary David Meiklejohn, first deputising for the Ibrox great in the 1927/28 season and gradually becoming a fixture in the first team. It was in 1931/32 that Simpson finally became the first choice centre half under Struth and it coincided with his first honour as he played a major role in the run to the Scottish Cup final, playing in every one of the seven ties up to and including the 3-0 win in the final replay against Kilmarnock.

It turned out to be the first of many medals for Simpson as a Rangers star. The following year he was a mainstay of the league championship winning team and of the league and Scottish Cup double winning side in 1933/34. That achievement was repeated in the next season when the two trophies remained in pride of place at Ibrox and Simpson was an ever-present in the successful defence of the Scottish Cup in 1935/36. He won his third First Division medal the following season and another in the 1938/39 campaign, the last before war stopped proceedings. Willie Woodburn was beginning to emerge as a natural successor at centre half when Simpson and so many of his football colleagues went off to war.

By then his impressive international career had also drawn to a close. It had begun in 1934 when he was first picked for his country and, despite defeat on his debut in Northern Ireland, he was promoted to the captain's role in his next appearance, and remained skipper through to his final game in dark blue in the closing weeks of 1937. During that time he made a total of fourteen appearances, scoring his one and only international goal against Czechoslovakia in his final year at that level. A fantastic record against the Auld Enemy was one of the key mementoes from his Scotland days, with Simpson holding the distinction of never losing against the English. In three matches, in all of which he served as captain, he notched two victories and a draw.

Simpson made two appearances in the 1939/40 season, one before the outbreak of war and one after, before calling time on his time as a Ranger. He could reflect on an amazing tenure in a light blue shirt and the type of devotion and dedication to the cause that marked him out as one of the club's greats.

Ulsterman Alex Stevenson was part of the RAF connection. He joined Rangers as a rookie teenager in 1930 and was part of Bill Struth's team by the 1932/33 season, playing a cameo role in the championship win that term with a single appearance. By the following term he was more involved, and started the campaign bang on form, scoring a hat-trick in a 9-1 trouncing of Ayr United at Ibrox on his way to seven goals in just eleven outings in the title win. His form won him international honours with Northern Ireland in the autumn of 1933 and, in turn, the attention of English clubs. Stevenson joined Everton early in 1934 and his intelligent play, coupled with expert ball skills, won him instant approval. He was a revelation playing alongside Dixie Dean and Tommy Lawton in that Toffees side, going on to win the championship in 1938/39. After the war he returned to play for Everton and took his record to ninety goals in 271 games before retiring from Goodison duty in 1949.

Many, many more men served club and country during that eventful period. The likes of Donald McLatchie and Thomas

Souter, who rose to become a captain with Royal Scots Fusiliers, as well as Alex McKillop and Tom McKillop are just a few. Like every workplace in Scotland, Ibrox waved farewell to employee after employee and hoped to see their like again when the hostilities came to an end.

14

GALLANTRY UNDER THE SICILIAN SUN

Willie Thornton, was a true playing legend with Rangers and a man who held a statesmanlike presence even after his boots had been hung up. Behind Thornton the star was Thornton the soldier and he served his country with the same aplomb as he served his club, winning the Military Medal for valour in the field to put his name among the heroes of his era.

It was in the winter of 1943 that the Ibrox legend's gallantry in the field was recognised, on the back of a spring and summer spent battling German and Italian forces. He was serving as a gunner in the 80th Medium Regiment of the Royal Artillery, formed from the Perthshire-based Scottish Horse regiment, and was involved at the heart of one of the Second World War's further flung operations. Rather than the muddy battlefields of France, it was in the southern territories of Italy that Thornton's heroics came to the fore.

A pre-war rising star at Ibrox, Thornton found a place in a new and different team when the fight against the Germans began, as he took his place in a developing regiment for a series of assignments that would test the British men to the very limit in unforgiving surroundings.

The 80th Medium Regiment departed from the UK in April

1943 and served with the 8th Army in North Africa before being rerouted as part of the major attack on a key strategic position on Italian soil: the sunshine island of Sicily. Now better known as a holiday destination shrouded in Mafia intrigue, the destination had totally different overtones for the Brits who landed on its shores in the 1940s. It was enemy territory and the scene for hard-fought battles against the twin-pronged armies of Germany and Italy.

Thornton had seen service in North Africa with his regiment and those campaigns had been the precursor to the Sicily deployment. British troops had defeated the Italians in Ethiopia in 1941 and the Italian-German coalition at El-Alamein in Egypt the following year. In 1943 hundreds of thousands of Italian soldiers were taken prisoner in Tunisia as Britain, with new support in the field from America, pushed home its superiority.

The success in Africa provided the springboard for the Allies to set their sights on the fringes of Europe, or the 'soft underbelly' of the continent, as it was described by British Prime Minister Winston Churchill. What followed was an incredible exercise in cunning and military strength.

Churchill and American President Franklin D. Roosevelt first decided upon the invasion of the southern Italian island of Sicily early in 1943 at the Casablanca Conference. The intention was to draw German forces away from France as well as sending a message to the enemy: the Allies were in the ascendancy.

The D-Day landings at Normandy would quickly overshadow events on Sicily, but at the time it marked the largest invasion by water ever seen in military conflict. Operation Husky, as it was codenamed, was on a scale that the German and Italian forces simply could not have predicted.

The British and US forces came together to invade with precision and pace. The British troops landed on the south-east of the island and the Americans on the south, working closely to give maximum impact rather than the original plan of hitting north and south at the same time.

More than 2,700 ships and landing vessels had gathered at Malta in preparation for the invasion, gathering from as far afield as the Clyde and Norfolk to Virginia in America.

The element of surprise was key to the whole operation. Even General Dwight D. Eisenhower and British counterpart Lord Louis Mountbatten, at their command post in Malta, only discovered the landing had taken place when they heard confirmation on BBC radio. The enemy forces were even more surprised, given the extent to which the intentions of the Allies had been disguised.

Operation Mincemeat has become part of the legend of the Second World War, the subject of books and much intrigue. It is worth revisiting, albeit briefly, to put the Sicilian landings in context and illustrate the planning that went into the campaign. It was in the spring of 1943 that the body of a British serviceman was planted off the coast of Spain. The real identity of the man in question was Glyndwr Michael, but the corpse had been carefully disguised to take on a new identity: Major William Martin, of the Royal Marines. He carried with him a briefcase containing papers outlining the Allied plans for an attack on Greece. Those plans were all part of the elaborate deception. As British intelligence had hoped, the body was recovered by the Spanish and the details, eventually, after more than a week of procrastination, passed to the German intelligence forces by their Spanish counterparts. The documents had been ingeniously removed from their envelopes, which had been complete with wax seals, to enable them to be copied by the Germans before being returned quickly to Spain's possession and being returned to their envelopes in time to be passed back to Britain's representatives by the Spaniards – with seemingly no trace that they had ever fallen into enemy hands.

Of course, they had. Unbeknown to the furtive Spanish authorities, Britain would have wanted it no other way. While Hitler and his chiefs readied themselves for the Greek offensive from British-led troops, they were unaware that they had fallen for the mother of all wartime hoaxes and were about to be hit with a surprise attack. Sicily had been mentioned in the carefully planted papers as a possibly decoy target, the perfect double bluff in a sense.

The letters had quickly found their way to the desk of Lieutenant-Colonel Alexis Baron von Roenne, one of Hitler's leading intelligence specialists. He signed off an assessment of the documents in May 1943, stating in the report: 'The circumstances of the discovery, together with the form and contents of the dispatches, are absolutely convincing proof of the reliability of the letters.'

While the paper trail was laying the foundations for the invasion, there was a more tangible process taking place in the skies above Sicily in the months prior to the arrival of the British troops. The island had been bombed sporadically by the RAF from late in 1942, something that in itself would not have appeared out of the ordinary at the height of the war. The cities of Palermo and Messina were badly hit, with infrastructure and military facilities targeted. While in hindsight it is clear there was a motive for disabling the capabilities of the enemy forces on Sicily, at the time the bombing raids were seen as little more than a show of strength, and a way of letting the Italian citizens know that all was not going their way in the conflict.

The islands of Lampedusa and Pantelleria, to the south of Sicily and with a key role as radar stations, were so successfully targeted that they were surrendered in June 1943 purely on the back of the aerial assault. It would be another month before the shock invasion of Sicily would be carried out.

The US Seventh Army, comprising around 200,000 troops,

and the British Eighth Army, adding a further 100,000 men, fell under the control of Eisenhower as Supreme Allied Commander for the operation. General Harold Alexander was in charge of the land invasion. It went largely to plan, with only minor difficulties encountered with getting the huge Allied force ashore together with the tons of equipment and artillery required for each squad of men.

Late on 9 July, and into the early hours of the following morning, the exercise swung into operation. By boat, landing craft and air, using parachutes and even gliders, the allied men landed on Sicily. Among that number was the brave Willie Thornton, with the twilight entry to Sicily a far cry from his experiences of running out in the full public glare of tens of thousands at Ibrox. Football must have been a distant memory as he faced up to the life and death exercise facing him and his colleagues from the Scottish Horse.

The fighting began as the German and Italian strategists hastily responded, not doing enough to prevent Syracuse, Ragusa and Noto falling under British control on the first day. The Italian resistance proved less dogged than that posed by the Germans, relying heavily on tanks and air power. They were rebuffed by a well-drilled and fiercely determined Allied force, and within days there was a drive to move inland.

Niscemi was captured by the Americans and the Brits took Vizzini, although there were spells of confusion surrounding the Allied strategy. Those were worked through by the troops on the ground and Caltanissetta was one of the next major towns to fall, with the US forces taking control on 18 July.

The following morning, on the mainland, Rome was bombed for the first time in the city's history. Within a week, Benito Mussolini had been removed from office and placed under protective arrest as the nation's king moved to have the dictator brought down from his position of power. With word filtering through of a looming humiliation for the Axis forces in Sicily, the first real signs of unrest were evident.

Back on Sicily, the British Eigthth Army found itself involved in a brutal battle on the Plain of Catania and in the Nebrodi Mountains, to the north-west of the famous Mount Etna.

As the final week of July loomed, the Americans were able to complete their charge into Palermo. There was little in the way of resistance from the Italian forces and large swathes of the public welcomed the Allied forces with open arms. Even the infamous Mafiosi on the island had promised their collaboration, vital to the smooth running of the operations on Sicily. Anglo-Italian families were liberated from fascist imprisonment as the campaign rumbled on.

Palermo, now a popular tourist destination renowned for its cultural diversity and as a cosmopolitan melting pot, had been conquered in the past by the Carthaginians, Greeks, Romans, Arabs, Normans, Angevins and Aragonese amongst others. The occupation by the Allied forces was different in that the Sicilians appeared disinclined to fight it. There were joyous scenes on the streets of Palermo as the trucks and jeeps of the US Army rolled into town.

All the time, the British forces were still fighting the more stubborn Germans, together with a token collection of Italian soldiers, on the Plain of Catania. The gains were slow and slight, but it was progress all the same as the frontline edged closer towards Messina over the Peloritan Mountains. The Germans, forced to concede defeat in Palermo, had redistributed troops to ensure the battle against the Brits was evenly matched.

By mid-August, the British forces were beyond Mount Etna and on 17 August the Germans and Italians evacuated their force of 100,000 men from the straits and the Allies had a path open to secure Messina. The battle had been won, although not without losses.

There were thousands of civilian deaths and casualties while around 5,000 Allied troops lost their lives. The split was closely balanced between the US and British armies, with just over 2,700 Brits killed. Around 16,000 Allied men were wounded or captured, with almost two-thirds of those belonging to British regiments who had been involved in the most intense warfare on the island. The enemy reported 29,000 killed or wounded, with around 140,000 captured by the Allies.

The events in Sicily were a catalyst for a seismic shift in Italian policy, with the nation switching sides to become an ally of Britain and the US on 8 September 1943. Within three years the fascist rule was a fading memory as the Italian Republic was born.

By the time Italy had switched sides, the Allies had already made a move on the mainland. Using Sicily as a base, they moved on Calabria early in September and then on to Taranto. There was a struggle to take Naples, but by October the Allies had a stronghold in the south of Italy, including Sardinia, where German troops had been withdrawn in the face of Allied occupation, and control of the seas around made for improved supply links and more tactical freedom. It also released naval resources, with the surrender of the Italian navy allowing Allied boats to switch their attention to events in Japan and elsewhere.

The pieces of the jigsaw were falling into place, with the foothold in the south of Italy also providing an opportunity to launch bombing attacks on the Balkan territories and northern Italy. That had been one of the prime objectives at the outset of the landing on Sicily and, despite reservations from the Americans about the plan to storm the island, it can be noted as one of the turning points in the Second World War away from the frontline in France. Although the Italian contribution was too little too late to be classed as a significant contribution to the Allied offensive, the added support provided an extra nudge for a campaign against the Germans that was gathering momentum day by day.

Despite difficulties along the way in terms of strategy once on the island, Operation Husky was lauded as a roaring success for the Allies. Lord Mountbatten had seen at first-hand the incredible strength mustered by the US and British forces in preparation for the invasion of Sicily and admitted he was awestruck by what he witnessed.

Mountbatten said:

I accompanied Admiral Ramsay on board the *Antwerp* and saw all the convoys as they passed on their way to their rendezvous south of Malta. I have been twenty-seven years at sea and I have never seen a sight like it in my life. It was like the Spithead Review multiplied by twenty. There were just forests of masts in every direction, as far as the eye could see. It was the most imposing and inspiring site, and all troops and sailors had their tails so obviously vertical that when you went anywhere near them they broke into cheers.

Accompanying Willie Thornton and the rest of the troops on those ships were the heavy duty weapons that the 80th Medium Regiment and the other Royal Artillery battle groups were equipped with.

Although still carrying the Scottish Horse name, his regiment had changed beyond all recognition from the one that had originally been granted that title when war was altogether less sophisticated.

The Scottish Horse Regiment can trace its beginnings back to the Boer War at the turn of the twentieth century, when Scots living in South Africa were pulled together to serve under the future Duke of Atholl. Further volunteers from Scotland and Australia were drafted in to form a second regiment.

In the First World War there were three regiments and they fought a dismounted role in Gallipoli and Egypt, with the soldiers firing from static positions after reaching their position on horseback. There had been mounted action on occasion, although accuracy while on horseback was significantly reduced.

The regiment served as cavalry scouts until 1939, by which time they became an artillery unit and formed the 79th and 80th Medium Regiments of the Royal Artillery. In 1956 there was an amalgamation with the Fife and Forfar Yeomanry, eventually becoming part of the Highland Yeomanry, Scottish Yeomanry and Queen's Own Yeomanry.

Horses had played a part in the First World War. Then there were tens of thousands of animals in the cavalry and, consequently, thousands of mounts were killed in action. Sacrifices had to be made in the pursuit of victory against the Germans and being able to cover the terrain of the frontline was central to the tactics. The horses came into their own during the First World War, with mechanisation of the military still in its early stages and the four-legged power proving vital in a whole host of roles.

The main purpose was as workhorses, quite literally. In the First World War the majority of artillery was dragged around the field by horse, and supplies of ammunition and provisions were also reliant on the effectiveness of the cavalry operation. The animals would be put to use day and night hauling loads from the holding areas deep within friendly territory to the very front of the line, within sight and firing distance of the enemy. It was dangerous and conspicuous work, but at the same time it was unavoidable if the battles were to be won and victory secured. Such was the demand for horses to aid the war effort that animals were called up from private ownership, something that obviously did not sit easily with the horse owners who had to hand over their beasts to the army. It was another example of the contribution that was required from all sections of society and the way in which everyday lives were turned upside down during that period as every resource, including the living and breathing, was poured into the fight against the German forces.

While the animals did the hard graft, they were of course simply tools at the disposal of their riders. The men of the cavalry were considered among the elite of the army and a string of senior officers could trace their roots back to those specialist arms of the force. Field Marshal Douglas Haig and General Allenby were just two of the officers who rose to prominence after serving in the cavalry and there was a certain prestige that accompanied the position in the ranks, something that ensured the cream of the military talent clamoured to be part of it.

While the pain of the loss of respected cavalry men was heartfelt, so too was the distress that the killing and maiming of the beloved horses caused to the troops who had to watch in horror as the innocent animals were dragged into the conflict and made to suffer amid the atrocities. It was not just the wounds and injuries inflicted by enemy fire that the horses were harmed by – a lack of adequate feed was another danger to the equine contingent, with exhaustion a common occurrence and the death toll high. Soldiers had no choice but to watch the trusty horses die in front of them.

Military thought changed quickly as mechanisation became a reality. At the turn of the twentieth century there was little doubt among the top brass that the charge of a horse was far more effective than the limited scope of a rifle. Even at the end of the Great War, Haig said:

I believe that the value of the horse and the opportunity for the horse in the future are likely to be as great as ever. Aeroplanes and tanks are only accessories to the men and the horse, and I feel sure that as time goes on you will find just as much use for the horse – the well-bred horse – as you have ever done in the past.

Yet already during the First World War the seeds had been sown for the elimination of the horse from battle. Machine guns made the opportunities to charge few and far between, leading to a reduction in the cavalry force as the war continued. Many men left to become infantry soldiers.

The use of horses was gradually phased out during the inter-war period, with the increasing use of motorised transport sounding the death knell for the humble horse as an army servant. In the late 1920s and throughout the 1930s there was a concerted effort to cut back the number of cavalry units, with only around 6,000 horses and 10,000 mules remaining in service going into the Second World War. The establishment of tank regiments had reduced the need for horses – but events in Italy, and particularly the rugged surroundings of Sicily, persuaded commanders to occasionally fall back upon the reliable sidekicks, mainly sourced locally where the animals were acclimatised and familiar with the territory.

For the men who had travelled from Britain, via Africa, to take part in the battles on Sicilian land there was no such opportunity to settle into their surroundings. They were plunged straight into action and emerged with great credit. Thornton was one of a number honoured for going above and beyond the call of duty during the short, sharp battle to take control of the island.

Throughout his life, Willie Thornton led an exemplary existence. A medal winner as a soldier, he was no stranger to silverware as a footballer either. He will always be remembered as one of the Ibrox elite, with a reputation befitting of a club that held the virtues of Bill Struth so dear during his time attached to Rangers.

It was Struth who first spotted the potential in Thornton in the 1930s, although it was during the post-war era that he would truly make his mark in a light blue shirt. As the 1950s dawned, he became the first Rangers striker to reach 100 goals in post-war football and his achievements in the box still mark him out as one of the greatest forwards ever to grace the turf.

Hailing from West Lothian, where he had been a schoolboy star, the striker was quickly welcomed into the Rangers family. By the age of sixteen he had signed as an amateur with the club and quickly progressed to turn professional as a first team player, making his debut in a single-goal victory against Partick Thistle early in 1937 and scoring his first goal just days later. The promising youngster was showing early signs of fulfilling his potential and quickly vindicated Struth's decision to fast-track him into the first eleven.

In his first season he made five appearances during the march to the championship and in the following campaign he turned out eighteen times. By 1938/39 he was deemed to have served his apprenticeship and was a near-permanent fixture in Struth's team, missing just a couple of games and scoring twenty-three goals while playing in tandem with Alex Venters. Those goals gave the teenage protégé his first senior medal as he helped his side to the First Division championship in considerable style, with Rangers streaking into a nine-point lead over challengers Celtic by the time the trophy was handed over. A huge part of the success that term was goalscoring prowess, with the Parkhead side not capable of matching the firepower in the Ibrox ranks.

Even at such a tender age, just eighteen when that memorable campaign kicked off, Thornton had proven himself as the complete centre forward. With exceptional control and a revered first touch, he was a man who could create opportunities as well as tuck them away. Add to the package renowned aerial ability and the picture of the complete centre forward becomes clear.

While the war years and the rigours of active service put many football careers to bed, Thornton returned from his army stint with the same tenacity and passion for the game as he had displayed during his breakthrough years with Rangers.

When Scottish football resumed in the summer of 1946 the striker was still only twenty-six. He slotted straight back into Struth's side as if he had never been away and his eighteen league goals helped the club to the 1946/47 championship, not to mention his six strikes en route to the Scottish Cup in the same season.

He was joint topscorer at Ibrox that year, tied with Jimmy Duncanson on twenty-five strikes in all competitions, and led the chart in his own right for four of the next five campaigns.

In that period he collected the Scottish Cup in 1947/48, the treble in 1948/49 and another league crown in 1950. A Scottish Cup winner's medal in the same year, when he scored a double in the 3-0 victory against East Fife, completed his glittering collection of prizes.

The trophy hat-trick in the historic 1948/49 term was aided in no small part by Thornton's wonderful contribution. It turned out to be the most prolific season of a fabulous career, bringing thirty-four goals in forty-three games across the First Division, Scottish Cup and League Cup. In the Scottish Cup the ratio was eight strikes in just five ties – including all three in the 3-0 victory against East Fife in the semi-final of the competition.

Joining those medals in the trophy cabinet were seven Scotland caps garnered over the course of a six-year international career. It began in 1946 when he made his debut in a 3-1 win against Switzerland and ended in 1952 following a 3-1 defeat in Sweden. Thornton's single goal in dark blue came just five days prior to his last outing, scoring in a 2-1 triumph in Denmark to add another proud achievement to his playing record.

On the pitch he was full energy and drive. Away from football, the great man enjoyed more relaxing pursuits, and he was not alone on that front.

Bill Struth famously nurtured a collection of plants in a greenhouse located behind the Broomloan Road terracing, the most sedate of past-times in the most unusual of surroundings. The fact the greenhouse and its panes of glass remained un-scathed through years of raucous football matches at the ground is testament to the good nature of the crowds of the era, and maybe fear of what would happen if the great man's oasis was ruined. While Struth's greenhouse has gone down in club folklore as a quirk of the time, what is less well known is that Struth was not the only budding horticulturist on the Ibrox staff.

Willie Thornton, a man who witnessed at first-hand the brutal and blood-curdling reality of war, was a hero on the battlefield, but away from the theatre of war there could have been no greater contrast. Long after the guns had been laid down, he could be found lovingly caring for the roses he cultivated. His enthusiasm for football was closely followed by his passion for his rose-growing hobby, passing on tips and knowledge to friends who shared his gardening past-time and passion for grafting stems to create new varieties of the flower. It was a gentle pursuit for one of the game's true gents.

After retiring from playing duty in 1952, the studious Thornton served as manager of Dundee and then Partick Thistle, stepping into the breach following the death of fellow Rangers legend David Meiklejohn in 1959 to embark on a nine-year reign at Firhill. He brought with him a wealth of experience and a calming influence and was hugely admired by the Jags board.

Only one club could have broken the partnership and that club was Rangers. When the Ibrox directors were looking for an experienced campaigner to work alongside rookie boss Davie White in 1968 they looked no further than Maryhill and Thornton agreed to return to his roots as part of a management team that included fellow army hero Harold Davis.

When White was dismissed in 1969 there was still a place at the club for Thornton, who was viewed as a valuable ally by incoming manager Willie Waddell.

For a generation of Rangers fanatics the combination of Waddell and Thornton in attack for the Gers, with Waddell's wing wizardry feeding his great friend with the type of gilt-edged chances he thrived on, had been a joy to behold. With their playing days behind them they reunited behind the scenes and laid the foundations for a decade of success in the 1970s.

Thornton became a trusted mentor to a new generation of light blue stars, always on hand with quiet words of encouragement and advice. Thornton was not brash and nor was he loud – but when he spoke he did so with the utmost authority. Right up to his passing, at the age of seventy-one, he was an inspiration to all who served the club he loved so dearly. He knew what it meant to be a Ranger and he was able to convey that ethos to all who fell under his wing, one of the last bastions of the Struth era and an upholder of the traditions that had been the bedrock of such wonderful success during his playing days.

When Thornton died in 1991 he was still an integral part of the football club, serving as custodian of the Ibrox trophy room and a guardian of the values intrinsic to day-to-day life at the club.

His passing left a void at the club and also removed another link to the proud past of the Scottish Horse Regiment he had served with such courage.

In 2009 a group of Thornton's former regimental colleagues

made an emotional return to Italy to pay their respects to fallen comrades and also to reflect on their good fortune. They were taken to the continent by the Italy Star Association, supported by lottery funding from the Heroes Return 2 programme making the trip possible.

At that time it was believed only four men from the Scottish Horse who had served in the Second World War remained alive. While the survivors are diminishing, it is certain that their achievements in Sicily will live long in military folklore.

15

THE WIZARD OF THE DRIBBLE

Who was the greatest footballer ever to grace the turf? Could it have been Rangers' very own Jim Baxter? Or does the title fall to the modern pretenders to the throne Lionel Messi, or Diego Maradona at his peak? Many would plump for Pele, some would vote George Best, and for those who can cast their mind back far enough there would be a few willing to hang their hat on Sir Stanley Matthews.

Baxter aside, only one of those world-famous figures has pulled on the famous light blue jersey and that man is Sir Stan. Matthews was a wartime guest for Rangers during one of the most tumultuous yet entertaining periods in football's colourful past.

Hopes were no doubt raised that Matthews may return in peace time and perch himself on the Ibrox wing permanently. In reality there was little prospect of that becoming a reality, despite the great man's fond memories of his briefest of dalliances with the Gers. The English legend always spoke with great affection about his Rangers days, although those who got to know him during his short time in the dressing room always maintained that Matthews would have been well out of the club's reach. Even then, wages and earning opportunities south of the border far outstripped what was on offer at Scottish clubs and there was no surprise when Matthews chose to resume his career with Stoke City.

The Wizard of the Dribble made his debut in Rangers colours on 30 March 1940, against Morton in the Scottish Regional League Western Division. He guested in the Number 7 shirt that had been worn with such distinction by Willie Waddell earlier in the season and helped his side to a 1-0 win, with Alex Venters scoring the only goal of the game in front of a crowd in excess of 20,000. It was the biggest gate at Ibrox, outside of the Old Firm showdown, that season. No doubt the new face added more than a handful to the numbers who poured through the turnstiles.

His next appearance was also in front of a healthy crowd, with 25,000 turning out for the final of the Glasgow Merchants' Charity Cup at Hampden in May that year. Matthews again patrolled his familiar right wing beat and again emerged on the winning side, with Partick Thistle beaten into the runners-up spot as Tory Gillick's double and another Venters goal did the damage. The Jags drew a blank and Rangers claimed the cup with a 3-0 win. Matthews, a man who was no stranger to the national stadium as a visiting England international, had seen the other side of the coin as he savoured the atmosphere of having the backing of the majority of the crowd in the ground for that day's game.

Tory Gillick was another guest on that occasion, even if he was a hugely familiar figure to the Ibrox crowd. He had returned north during the war years and, although an Everton player, was allowed to pull on the blue of his home city club on a number of occasions.

Matthews was very much at his peak when he turned out for Rangers. He had made his debut for Stoke City, his home town team, in 1932 as a seventeen-year-old. He emerged as a star for the Potteries side as well as for England. Arguably, war robbed

Matthews of the chance to fulfil his full potential, although Stoke's loss proved to be a decent gain for a string of clubs who took advantage of his wartime availability. Rangers were not the only side on Matthews' CV during that period as he also turned out for Manchester United, Crewe and Blackpool. His link to the Seasiders had come through the RAF, having been posted to the Lancashire coast in his role as a P.T. instructor. He and his wife enjoyed Blackpool life and settled in the area when they bought a small hotel.

While he got his teeth into air force commitments and his new life, Matthews kept himself match sharp by turning out in various wartime games and competitions. He made several appearances north of the border, including for a Scottish Select side in Aberdeen in 1941 against a Scottish Command Select and another in the Granite City four years later for an RAF side against the Dons.

His tartan tasters left a lasting impression on the famous flanker, who when asked more than half a century later to pick out the stars of that era in the Scottish game plumped for three Ibrox men.

The first was Jimmy Caskie, a man he knew from English football and his starring role with Everton. Caskie was another of the men to guest for Rangers during the war and he eventually made the move to Ibrox permanent. The second was a man that Matthews had the pleasure of playing alongside in Rangers colours twice. That was Willie Thornton, a player who everyone at Ibrox knew all about but who proved a revelation to the England star when he joined him in the same forward line for those fleeting occasions. The final individual singled out by Matthews was George Young.

By the time Young made his mark, Matthews was safely back on familiar territory and putting his stamp on the English domestic scene. He switched to Blackpool in 1947 and six years later led the Bloomfield Road side to the FA Cup in what has become known simply as the Matthews Final. In 1956 he collected the first ever European footballer of the year title, eventually being knighted in the same year he played his final game as a fifty-year-old in 1965. It was the final chapter in an incredible story and one which touched Ibrox, albeit briefly.

He emigrated to Canada for a spell after retiring from the game, returning to England prior to his death in 2000. Even during his exile he continued to follow the British game and, between lamenting the lack of personalities in the modern game, was heard to extol the virtues of a certain Alistair McCoist. It seems the Light Blues did indeed make a lasting impression on Sir Stanley.

The cameo from Stanley Matthews is just one of the quirks thrown up by the Second World War period. Another is perhaps the most bizarre claim to fame that Rangers can pin their name to – that of prisoner-of-war camp champions. It has been reported that a competition staged in a prisoner-of-war camp in Germany in 1942 had seen fourteen teams, each carrying the name of an English or Scottish side, compete. It was the honorary Rangers who came out on top of the pile, pipping Preston North End to the title. For the record, Everton won the cup in the makeshift British tourney.

The team also dominated in more regular competition back in Scotland during the six years of turmoil. While a clutch of Ibrox players found work in reserved occupations in the Clyde shipyards, working in engineering and munitions, there were as many out on active service.

That made team selections understandably unpredictable and player availability sporadic, something all teams were having to contend with. Rangers coped better than any other side and came through the adversity to give some rare moments of distraction amid the austerity and gloom of the war.

Some have put Rangers' success down to the number of players who were retained close to home in those reserved occupations, but that claim falls down with even the most cursory of examinations. Would a team playing the system to bolster its chances of success end up having to play their established wing half, Scot Symon, in goal for an entire match because no keeper was available to play? That is exactly what happened in the spring of 1942 when the future Gers manager pulled on the Number 1 shirt in an extraordinary 8-2 victory at Clyde.

By then the Light Blues were already firmly ensconced as the team to beat, leading the pack throughout the period having kicked off by winning the Scottish Regional League Western Division when it was hastily pulled together in the 1939/40 season after the First Division was abandoned due to war.

Scotland had been quick to rip up the traditional rule book and move to a more manageable and less grand football set-up. The new look was part by design and part by necessity, since the British government had banned all entertainment venues from operating within days of war being declared. In those heady days, when there were genuine world-class talents being produced in Scotland, football could be considered *the* entertainment of choice for the working man.

While the SFA cancelled all player contracts, they allowed clubs to retain registrations of individuals in preparation for peace time. Few could have anticipated how far away normality would prove.

By way of compromise, football supporters were promised their action fix by means of a decision to allow friendly fixtures to be played. There were notable exceptions however, with Glasgow and Clydebank among the towns and cities on the banned list due to the anticipation of bombing raids by the Germans.

As it happened, a swift resolution to the football quandary was hit upon by Scottish office bearers. The league proper had been abandoned on 13 September 1939, and eight days later a plan to create a system of regional leagues was rubber-stamped by the government. There was a month's break before the action began, allowing organisers time to piece together the finer details and consider logistics for the wartime effort.

The agreed proposals included two leagues of sixteen clubs, controversial at the time because it led to six clubs losing their place among the senior sides. There was even more disquiet surrounding the financial arrangements, which led to hardship for the clubs from the east as they missed out on money-spinning fixtures against the Old Firm. It was a different era, but there were very familiar arguments against league recon-struction, and strong echoes of the reasoning behind the smaller sides vetoing a switch to a ten-team top flight in 2011.

The figures were smaller but still significant at the time. Hearts pointed towards annual losses of £2,500 as one of the reasons for aiming for a swift return to the previous set-up, although their argument was undone slightly by the fact that Celtic's deficit was almost three times that figure after the revamp took place.

There had been murmurs that the league would return to normal by the summer of 1940, but the heightened fighting on the frontline led to a decision in June that year that the regio-nalised basis would continue until the war ended.

It was tweaked slightly, with Rangers taking their place in the newly named Southern League, and a League Cup was intro-duced to supplement the Scottish Cup and boost the fixture count for the cash-strapped clubs. The Summer Cup was also created to bring year-round football to Scotland for the first time.

The end of the war in 1945 did not bring an immediate return to normal league football, with the Southern League running for one further season. Guest players of the war years faded into the memory banks as the regular players filtered back into Scotland to take their place back in their club colours. Many were not fortunate enough to return from war, but the brutal reality of that period is that life, and sport, had to go on for those who did survive.

Rangers emerged from the troubles in a strong position. Bill Struth's side coasted to victory in the regional league in 1939/40 and added the Scottish Emergency War Cup when Dundee United were defeated 1-0 in the final thanks to a Jimmy Smith goal.

It was a similar story in the 1940/41 campaign when the newly formed Southern League was clinched, albeit by just a three-point margin from Glasgow rivals Clyde. Cup competition took the form of the Southern League Cup, and again the silverware was bound for Govan as Hearts were beaten 4-2 in the final replay at Hampden after the original tie had been drawn 1-1. Among the goalscorers that day was Willie Thornton, making one of only six appearances that term due to his army commitments. He had lost none of his ability, scoring three goals in those half dozen matches.

The Southern League Cup was retained in 1941/42, when guest Tory Gillick scored the only goal of the game against Morton in the final, and the Southern League was clinched again, this time Hibs the closest challengers. The Easter Road side were eight points adrift when the final whistle sounded.

A Southern League and cup double followed in 1942/43, with the cup returning to Ibrox by virtue of a corner tally of eleven to Falkirk's three in the final after the scores were locked at 1-1. It was a bizarre way to win a competition but fortunes were reversed in 1943/44 when Hibs lifted the Southern League Cup with a superior flag kick count of six to Rangers' five after a goalless final. Still, Struth could console himself with the fact his charges had once again marched to the Southern League title with a seven-point lead over Celtic.

As the war raged on, so too did the players called on to pull on the light blue shirt. The 1944/45 season brought more Southern League joy, when Celtic again were left to console themselves with the runners-up berth, and the Southern League Cup was brought back to Ibrox courtesy of a 2-1 victory over Motherwell.

The league title in 1945/46, a campaign in which Rangers lost the cup final 3-2 to an emerging Aberdeen side, rounded off the war years' effort and set the club up for a tilt at domestic honours when the traditional football programme resumed in the summer of 1946.

The light coming from the dark days of the war came in the shape of a new group of players hungry to emulate the success of their more experienced colleagues – players such as George Young, the most notable of the young men who debuted during the wartime competitions and went on to star in the 1940s and '50s. It was a transitional period as Struth began to introduce new blood to his team, but the experience of the old guard would be just as important in the years ahead. The success of the war years was the springboard to so many of the achievements that followed, starting with the league and League Cup double in 1946/47, and continuing with the Scottish Cup win the following term, the famous domestic treble of 1948/49 and another league and Scottish Cup double in 1949/50 to sign off from the 1940s in considerable style.

The joy of the football public was palpable as normal service resumed. Crowds during the war years had been limited for a litany of reasons, but by the time the curtain rose on the 1946/47 term the supporters were flooding back in their tens of thousands. The first home game, a league encounter with championship rivals Hibs, attracted 50,000 while gates of 60,000 against Aberdeen and 85,000 for the home Old Firm encounter proved that football was bouncing back stronger than ever before. Success on and off the park gave Rangers many reasons to be cheerful and spirits were soaring among players, staff and fans alike.

Even during the dark days the supporters had rallied around when called upon to boost the war effort. Football had a role to play as a vehicle for fundraising during the Second World War as well as a form of entertainment and relief. A series of benefit matches were played to capitalise on Rangers' popularity and help boost the coffers of deserving causes.

The first of those games fell on 1 April 1941, at Ibrox, when an RAF team visited Govan to play in the Sir Archibald Sinclair Cup. As Secretary of State for Air, Sinclair, leader of the Liberal Party, had given his name to the trophy. He was no stranger to the city in which the competition was played, having served as rector of Glasgow University for a seven-year term following his election in 1938.

Proceeds were to go to the Clydeside Air Raid Distress Fund and the light blue legions did not let the side down – a gate of 25,500 ensured the exercise was valuable to the war effort.

On the pitch, Rangers were less charitable. The visiting airmen put up a good fight but fell to a 3-2 defeat as goals from Alex Venters, Charlie Johnston and Jimmy Smith kept the home fans smiling in keeping with their helping to keep the cash boxes jingling.

Indeed, the fund survived well past the war. In 2003 Argyll and Bute Council set about deciding how to best distribute the remaining cash held in the Clydeside Air Raid Distress account, with the balance sitting at £2,523 at that time. It was during a period of rationalisation of a whole host of obscure trust funds held by the local authority.

The 1941/42 season brought a further two challenge matches with a fundraising aim. The first was on 27 August 1941, and was played at Somerset Park in Ayr, hosted by the Ayr County Council to boost its war fund. A crowd of 4,000 filtered into the little ground to watch the giants from Ibrox take on a British Army side that had travelled north for the game. It ended in an honourable draw, both sides notching two goals with the Rangers double coming from Charlie Johnston and Tory Gillick.

Just days later there was another benefit match, this time in the familiar surroundings of Ibrox. Preston North End, that most famous of English names, provided the opposition as the club did its bit for the Lord Provost's Central Relief Fund. On 1 September 1941, a crowd of 35,000 assembled to see the visitors outclassed by their Scottish opponents, beaten 3-1 as Gillick, Jimmy Smith and Willie McIntosh did the business.

The match provided a welcome boost for the relief fund, which had been called upon to bridge a variety of financial gaps during the war years. One of the most high-profile drains on the fund came following the sinking of the *Athenia* during a voyage from Glasgow to Montreal in September 1939.

The ship, built on Clydeside at the Fairfield yard for the Donaldson line, became the first merchant marine casualty of the conflict when she was torpedoed by the Germans 200 miles west of the Hebrides – just ten hours after war had been declared by Britain. Of 1,418 on board there were 112 deaths. Many of those rescued were brought back ashore at Greenock and put up in Glasgow hotels, funded by the relief fund and assisted by a £1,000 donation from the Donaldson line, as well as a £250 contribution from Fairfield.

While Scottish and English football was quickly put on the back burner during the war years, and supporters had to survive on a ration of challenge matches and low-key regional competitions, the German public were still being treated to business as usual.

The sport was seen as a propaganda vehicle by Hitler and his henchmen, desperate to avoid any sign of weakness or disruption following their move into Poland, and very much intent on keeping up appearances for a nation of fans who had always been passionate about the sport. For several years the Germans managed to maintain competitive football, eventually seeing the impact of their military folly when the leagues, in a microcosm of what was happening in the country as a whole, began to fall to pieces.

One of the reasons the Germans were able to continue without significant change in the early days of the First and Second World Wars was that they already had a head start on the Brits. While Scottish authorities set about hastily arranging regionalised leagues, in Germany that system had long been in place.

Winners of the district tournaments would gather together for end-of-season play-offs, in both league and cup, and that was well suited to wartime football. It took until the 1960s for the national Bundesliga to be put in place – by which time Germany had already demonstrated its ability to bounce back from the turmoil the nation had endured in the 1940s by sweeping to victory in the 1954 World Cup final.

When war broke out, it was Schalke who were the team to beat in the German game. They won the championship in 1940, pipping that year's cup winners Dresden to the title. Nuremberg, defeated cup finalists in 1940, were among the other major players at the time while Rapid Vienna, part of the domestic scene by virtue of Austria falling under German control, also tasted success when they won the cup in 1941. Suggestions have been made that Rapid's moment in the spotlight was politically motivated; the Viennese overcoming a three-goal deficit against Schalke to come back and secure a win was an excellent public relations boost for the German administration as they attempted to bring the Austrian public onside. Munich 1860 also won the cup, in 1942, while Schalke continued to dominate league proceedings.

It was then that the football scene in Germany began to descend into chaos as the requirement for additional military manpower began to strip away the sporting talent for more laborious action in the trenches. It took longer for German football to return to normality post-war, with the competitions regaining their familiar look in the summer of 1947 after years in a state of flux. Given the World Cup outcome seven years later, the break clearly did little long-term damage to the country's standing on the global football stage.

16

KEEPING THE FLAG FLYING

The end of the Second World War did not sever the Rangers links with the forces. Indeed, a succession of Ibrox teams benefited from the discipline and courage the British Army instilled in men who rose to become guiding lights to the next generation of light blue stars.

Willie Thornton was one of the trailblazers as he returned from service to take on a mentoring role under Davie White and Willie Waddell in the 1960s and '70s. The iron-willed figure of Harold Davis followed in his bootsteps when he joined the coaching staff in the 1960s. As a player, Davis took no prisoners. As a coach he became an influential figure. As a soldier, his story was inspirational.

He was part of a generation too young to have seen service in the Second World War, but the end of the battle against Hitler's Germany did not mark the end of active duty for the British Army. There were still threats to be addressed and conflicts to be resolved across the world, and a changing of the guard was required as the forces set about recruiting a new breed of soldiers with fresh legs and the same fierce loyalty to the cause. Scotland continued to be a fertile recruitment ground.

Davis, long before he rose to become a star of the domestic and European game as a Rangers man, was part of that new intake as he put himself forward for duty in an army that had gone through a strength-sapping yet morale-boosting triumph against the Nazis. He was exactly the type of character required and he set about launching his army career with the type of strength and fortitude that would later transfer to the Ibrox turf as he established himself as a favourite among the light blue loyal with his relentless dedication to the cause.

It was his experience of war that made the achievements in football all the more remarkable for Davis. He fell under enemy fire during the Korean War in 1952 and spent a year coura-geously battling back from his injuries to defy medics and embark on a career as a professional sportsman. He had not been expected to live, let alone go on to play football at the very highest level.

American medical teams patched him up in Korea and spells in hospital in Japan and then Scotland followed. After eighteen operations and a determined spell of rehabilitation, Davis was ready to reignite his football career that had begun before his spell of service with the Black Watch in Asia. It had been a long and painful road back to full fitness and one travelled with the type of commitment that became a hallmark of Davis through-out his career.

He had been a promising player with East Fife when he joined the army, having grown up in the Fife town of Cupar. His manager in Methil was Scot Symon, and it was Symon, by then in charge at Rangers, who gave him a passport back into top-flight football. In 1956, after being convinced war wounds were no barrier to Davis' successful comeback, Symons took him to Ibrox. It was a massive gamble, but one that paid off in spectacular fashion for the shrewd coach.

Renowned as one of the game's toughest competitors and fittest players, Davis went on to give years of sterling service as a player and hoovered up a string of honours along the way.

Davis went on to play out his days with Partick Thistle and coached Queen's Park as successor to Eddie Turnbull in the 1960s before being lured back to Ibrox as part of Davie White's coaching staff. The inexperienced White had seen the merit in falling back on the considerable experience and stature of Davis. White, a rising star of the Scottish coaching scene, had his growing stock to his credit, but the fear was that he would struggle to gain respect in a Rangers dressing room packed with medal-winning international stars.

Respect was something that Davis had never struggled to attract. A gentleman off the park but a born winner as a sportsman, he was an ideal foil for a rookie manager with no tangible connection to Ibrox prior to his appointment. Beside him he had a man who lived and breathed Rangers.

While the experiment with White proved ultimately unsuccessful for the Rangers board, the partnership with Davis did not end when time was called on his tenure as Ibrox boss. The two were reunited for a successful spell at Dundee in the 1970s, defeating Celtic in the League Cup final in 1973 to bring a smile to a proud Rangers man's face. Davis went on to put himself in a self-imposed exile from football, calling time on his coaching career to head north and forge a long and successful career as a hotelier in the Highlands before retiring to enjoy the good life, retaining his links to Rangers as a popular figure both at Ibrox and at various functions the length and breadth of the country.

All of those milestones, achievements and memories in football would not have been possible had it not been for the quick thinking of the medics who saved his life all those years ago on a foreign battlefield. He was almost killed fighting for another country's freedom.

Britain felt a duty to play its part, given the complex set of circumstances surrounding the war in which Davis found himself pitched into. The Korean War bore its roots in the uneasy political and military situation left by the end of the Second World War. The future of the Japanese empire had been decided at Allied summit meetings and Korea, one of Japan's colonies since 1910, was part of that solution. The north of the island was to be occupied by Soviet Russia and the south run by a US administration pending a return to independence.

In the aftermath of the Second World War the Soviets supported the Stalinist regime under Kim Il-sung and created the North Korean People's Army, equipped with Russian tanks and artillery. In the South, the presidency of Syngman Rhee sought national unity by force. The American-trained South Korean military were, in comparison to their northern neighbours, poorly equipped for serious combat. Sensing weakness, the North Koreans invaded the Republic of Korea on 25 June 1950, on the back of years of border skirmishes.

In response, the Security Council invoked the United Nations Charter and branded the North Koreans as aggressors. Member states were called on to send in military assistance and American and British troops were sent into action.

As the North Koreans advanced rapidly south, aiming to take the vital port of Pusan, the Americans dug in as they awaited reinforcements. In mid-September, two divisions landed well to the enemy rear at the port of Inchon. With their communications cut and aerial bombardments raining in, the North Koreans fled back to their own territory. They were pursued, sparking communist China into life and, after a powerful UN offensive in November, the Chinese sent their armies in.

The UN forces recoiled in disorder and, by the new year, were defending a line well to the south of Seoul, the capital of South Korea. Morale was low but the new field commander, General Ridgway, began to forge minor advances early in 1951.

By mid-April, the Allies were back in the area of the border when the Chinese launched their spring offensive. The UN stood firm and for two years the border saw dogged fighting that brought little in the way of advances for either side.

Heavily fortified positions, using artillery, mines and wire to deny the enemy access to strategically important ground, ensured it became a tactical, long-term engagement.

The fight for air superiority became crucial. The US Air Force, with B-29 bombers and American fighters, went against Russian-built MiG-15 fighters piloted by the Chinese crews. The introduction of the F-86 Sabre fighters by the US gave the UN forces the advantage in the world's first ever supersonic air combats. At sea, the Allies enjoyed total supremacy when the North Korean torpedo boats were scuppered.

By the middle of 1951, with the action on the ground locked and showing no sign of breaking, the armistice talks began. They would stretch on for a further two years, with the future of the communist prisoners the main stumbling block as many were unwilling to be repatriated to the North as was being demanded by their own country. Eventually a solution was agreed upon and in July 1953 silence fell over the battlefields. Operation Big Switch saw thousands of former prisoners on each side returned.

Around 100,000 Brits served in the Japan-Korea theatre during the war. The American Department of Defence put its death toll at close to 40,000, while Britain lost 1,078 and saw 2,674 wounded and a further 1,060 classed as missing or taken prisoner.

The true casualty figures for the North and South Koreans and Chinese will never be known. It is estimated that some 46,000 South Korean soldiers were killed and over 100,000 wounded. The Chinese are estimated by the Pentagon to have lost over 400,000 killed, a further 486,000 wounded and 21,000 captured. The North Koreans lost about 215,000 killed, had 303,000 wounded and over 106,000 captured or posted missing.

It was a brutal and unforgiving war that brought heavy losses. From a British standpoint the positive to emerge from the conflict was the glowing praise for the skills and conduct of its forces, who combined with Commonwealth colleagues from Australia, New Zealand and Canada with efficiency and heart. Since 1953, the Republic of Korea has gone from strength to strength and taken its place in modern society. The North has remained mired in its Stalinist roots and the concept of unity remains a distant dream for the population of an island that continues to live in the shadow of military threat and menace from the north.

Davis, a man who still bears the scars of that protracted conflict, can reflect with satisfaction on his contribution to the British effort in Korea. He remembers all too vividly the men he served alongside – and those who were not fortunate enough to return.

Proud of his military background, having followed his father's lead in serving in the army, the Ibrox legend is an enthusiastic supporter of the Erskine and its efforts to support Scotland's servicemen and women. As one of the club's surviving war heroes, he is the perfect figurehead and a living example of the positive story of war and hope for casualties even today. With support, expert care and a very large dose of determination there is always a chance to recover from severe injury to return to civilian life. In the case of Davis, civilian life afforded him the opportunity to live his dream and pull on the famous light blue jersey time after time.

One of the most famous servicemen to serve on the Ibrox staff never got that opportunity, having arrived at Ibrox when his playing days were behind him. That did not stop Jock Wallace from making his indelible mark on the club and its support with a regime that would undoubtedly have had far less impact had it not been for his military experience.

Wallace, the man known as Jungle Fighter, brought his army expertise to the fore as coach and then manager at Ibrox. His legendary training regimes, credited with making the Rangers squad of the 1970s the fittest in the country, owed much to his experience in the army.

Wallace spent three years with the King's Own Scottish Borderers in the 1950s, and his service took him into one of the harshest environments – the jungle of Malaya. Having been pressed into service in Northern Ireland in the early 1950s, Wallace's regiment shifted to Malaya in 1955 and embarked upon three years of operations against communist forces as they fought for the country's freedom during what was known as the Malayan Emergency. The sacrifices of the Scottish soldiers proved worthwhile, with the nation prospering in the years that followed the successful campaign.

The Malayan Emergency, broadly running between 1948 and 1960, stemmed from the formation of the Federation of Malaya in 1948 following World War Two. The territory had been formed by unifying various British territories, but the Communist Party of Malaya, primarily Chinese, was opposed to the principle of the democratically governed state. The party began its fight soon after the formation of the federation, and in June 1948 the government declared a state of emergency. By the mid-1950s, after concerted British efforts both politically and in military action, the rebels had been pushed into a corner on both fronts. However, it was not until the turn of the 1960s that the emergency was officially brought to an end.

The fighting at the height of the emergency was intense against an enemy better suited to the climate and terrain. The conditions in the dense jungle were strength sapping for the Brits sent in. Wallace, with his sporting background, as a goalkeeper of some repute, proved up to the task and was invigorated by the bravery of his comrades and the strength of character and physical power they displayed in this most alien of surroundings.

He spent eighteen months in those testing circumstances and once reflected: 'You soon discovered the men who had bottle and could do the business. All the men I knew in that category came back and did something with their lives.'

There is no doubting that Wallace went on to do something with his life. He lived his dream late in life, having had to concede defeat in his hopes to make it to Ibrox as a player. He was a Rangers fanatic as a schoolboy growing up in Wallyford, in East Lothian, but his playing career took him south rather than west.

Wallace featured for Workington, Ashton-under-Lyme, Berwick Rangers, West Brom, Bedford, Hereford and Airdrie. In that time he famously shut out his Ibrox heroes while player-manager of Berwick Rangers in the 1-0 Scottish Cup win over Rangers in 1967.

That success gained him an opportunity to move to Hearts as assistant manager the following year, and by 1969 his rapid coaching rise took another giant leap when he was taken to Ibrox by Willie Waddell to lead the first team.

He immediately set about focusing on stamina and conditioning. The notorious sessions on the Gullane sands were just a small part of a programme that challenged his charges day in and day out, testing them to the absolute limit of their physical capabilities.

A succession of stars of the 1970s went on to play well into what should have been the twilight years of their career, with the majority crediting the schooling they received under Wallace as the catalyst for their longevity. Sandy Jardine, voted Scotland's player of the year at the grand old age of thirty-seven in 1986, was perhaps the most notable example, but there were many others who enjoyed extended spells at the top level after working with Wallace and adhering to his military-style programmes. Tommy McLean and Alex MacDonald, both patrolling stamina-sapping beats in the midfield, were others who made a mockery of the theory that turning thirty marked the beginning of the end for a top-level player. Whether it was on field trips to daunting training locations or during the daily work-outs in and around Ibrox, there was a respect for Wallace's near-obsessive focus on fitness and strength among the squads who fell under his charge during his long association with Rangers.

Those who served under Wallace, and even those who en-countered him as outsiders, speak of a fearsome character with a steely single-minded nature. Undoubtedly his military service had a bearing on his approach and, having seen at first-hand the leadership that pulled his regiment together, he set about creating a culture of discipline and rigid structure at Ibrox.

In June 1972 he earned promotion to the top job as Waddell's successor, and the rest is history. With his bombastic personality and insatiable appetite for success, Wallace went on to end Celtic's domination and give the Bears a series of trophy-laden years. His fighting spirit manifested itself in his team selection, recruiting players, including Tam Forsyth notably, who added battling qualities to his squad.

Wallace won his first honour with a 3-2 win over Celtic in the 1973 Scottish Cup final. In the 1974/75 season the championship was claimed for the first time since 1964. The Treble was claimed in 1976 and again in 1978 before Wallace stunned Scottish football by resigning in the aftermath of that second clean sweep. He went on to lead Leicester City after apparently falling out with the Ibrox board over the terms on offer.

In 1982 he returned to Scotland to take charge of Motherwell and the following year was back at his spiritual home in Govan as he embarked on a second stint as Rangers manager. He won the League Cup in the season of his return and again in 1984/85, but the following campaign was fruitless and Wallace departed. Football was changing, Rangers was changing. Wallace was out and in his place came Graeme Souness and an Ibrox revolution built upon the type of financial resources that his predecessor could not have expected to have at his disposal even in his wildest dreams. What Wallace lacked in cash he had to make up for in other ways, and his strength of character was his currency.

After the disappointment of his second spell at Ibrox, the gruff coach dusted himself down and looked for new opportunities. He found them in an unlikely setting, being appointed Seville manager in 1987 to add another slice of intrigue to a fascinating story. He spent a year in Spain and also served with Colchester in the late 1980s. Wallace died in 1996 at the age of sixty-one.

17

THE LEGACY

Every second week 50,000 Rangers supporters file into Ibrox to take their seat in the plush surroundings of the modern ground to watch the millionaires of Ally McCoist's first team ply their trade in front of television cameras beaming footage of Gers games to all corners of the globe. The contrast between today's game and the one played by the heroes of both world wars could not be greater. Few who attend today's SPL encounters can hark back to the post-war era of the late 1940s, let alone the inter-war decades of the '20s and '30s. Yet, today's Rangers supporters have joined together in their thousands to prove that the Ibrox loyal will never forget the veterans who gave their all for their country.

More than £260,000 has been raised and passed to Erskine, the charity dedicated to caring for Scotland's ex-servicemen and women, through unstinting support for the Rangers Supporters Erskine Appeal. From charity walks to sportsman's dinners, events big and small have combined to push the running total through that magic mark.

The appeal has captured the imagination not just of supporters of a certain vintage, but also of the new breed, the iPod generation. In April 2011 the reach of the Erskine effort shot into the headlines when the Ibrox anthem *Penny Arcade* raced to the top of the HMV download music chart on the back of rousing renditions by the Bears during the championship-winning season.

The classic Sammy King pop song, best known for the Roy Orbison version that reached number twenty-seven in the UK singles chart in 1969, was adopted with vigour by the light blue legions, and enterprising fans Alex Hamilton and Simon Leslie set about turning that to Erskine's advantage.

Hamilton, who works in the music industry, tracked down King to his home in Yorkshire, and the songwriter, himself an ardent football fan and Huddersfield Town season ticket holder, agreed to allow his version of the song to be released for digital download with proceeds to be donated to Erskine.

With his seventieth birthday looming, it was an unexpected moment in the spotlight for a musician who retired in 2007 to concentrate on lowering his golf handicap and follow his beloved Town. In his prime, King had shared the stage with the Beatles, the Rolling Stones and Orbison himself. In his dotage King took centre stage at Ibrox as VIP guest of the club towards the end of the 2010/11 season in recognition of his generous gesture. He listened as his tune was belted out from all four sides of the stadium and no doubt let his mind drift back to the heady days of the Swinging Sixties.

The response to the single was phenomenal and the chart-topping flood of downloads was the icing on the cake. The Penny Arcade effort coincided with the ninety-fifth anniversary of Erskine, as well as the ninety-fifth anniversary of the Battle of the Somme. More currently, it also tied in with the return of the 2 Scot Regiment from service in Afghanistan.

Rangers fans launched the official Erskine effort in 2007 and have been determined in their pursuit of bolstering the charity's resources. The modest initial aim was to pull in a useful £1,000 donation for one particular ex-services home in Bishopton. The ball started rolling and hasn't stopped, with money continuing to flood in through collections, events and websites.

The giving is not without necessity. It has been estimated that it costs £21,000 every day to keep Erskine's well-oiled machine rolling. Not surprisingly, every penny raised is appreciated by the team responsible for running an organisation that provides lifeline services throughout Scotland.

The charity provides a host of services to its residents: from physiotherapy to speech therapy and from podiatry to full medical care. Whatever is required by those who fall under Erskine's wing, there is a will to provide it. And where there's a will, there's a way.

The dedicated care homes lie in Edinburgh, Anniesland, Bishopton and Erskine. Outside of those areas, veterans benefit from a bursary scheme which enables them to receive care at partnership homes in Aberdeen, Inverness, Perth, Dundee and Dumfries. Wherever the service is provided the aim is the same – to provide former service personnel with the care and attention they deserve.

Every Erskine centre has its own personality. In Edinburgh a purpose-built care home on Gilmerton Road provides twenty-four hour nursing care for fifty-four residents and dementia care for twenty-two residents. In addition there is provision at the Personnel Recovery Centre to treat troops wounded on current operations in close proximity to the garrison in the city.

The Personnel Recovery Centre was the first of its kind in Britain and opened its doors in 2009. It was created in conjunction with fellow forces charity Help for Heroes and the army itself. The residential wing of the centre is named after Corporal Mark Wright GC, who was killed in 2006 in Afghanistan's Helmand Province when a routine patrol encountered an unmarked minefield. He was posthumously awarded the George Cross in recognition of the courage he displayed during the incident.

Erskine received a huge boost in 2011 when the Royal British Legion announced a £5 million grant for the facility, covering the running costs through to 2020. Between its creation in 2009 and that association with the legion less than two years later, the PRC treated fifty-seven soldiers and was held up as a shining example of a facility which it is hoped will be used as a blueprint for similar centres throughout Britain.

In the west, Erskine Park opened in 2006 at Bishopton. The forty-room facility boasts its own activity centre with a recreation coordinator, and has close links to the nearby Erskine Home, which sits in a country setting in the shadow of the Erskine Bridge. The £16 million Erskine Home opened its doors in 2000 and can cater for 180 residents, providing nursing and dementia care on a long-term and respite basis. Prince Charles performed the ceremonial duties, taking his lead from his great-great aunt, Princess Louise.

Erskine Mains, in the heart of the town, also opened in 2000 and is home to thirty-four residents while Erskine Glasgow, on the site of the former Flanders House, opened in 2007 at Anniesland and has forty-six beds.

The charity also has fifty-seven cottages for ex-servicemen and women and their families to live in independently. Initially let to veterans for free, the properties now carry a nominal rent to support an ongoing building programme that has seen new homes spring up to supplement the existing estate and replace the older homes. In 2009 a programme was launched to rebuild all of the cottages on the Erskine site at Bishopton and the project is expected to run for four years.

At every site the underlying ethos is first-class care and attention for each and every one of the residents, with more than 75,000 men and women benefiting from the organisation's work since its inception early in the twentieth century.

It was in October 1916 that the Erskine Hospital, then known as the Princess Louise Scottish Hospital for Limbless Sailors and Soldiers, opened. A large proportion of the money to create the facility came from public donations as the Scottish conscience was pricked by reports of the brutality in the field during the Great War and the first-hand experience of the death and casualties being inflicted on the families of the fallen young men. More than £100,000 was raised to make the plan a reality.

Thomson Aikman, the owner of the Mansion House of Erskine on a peaceful site on the banks of the River Clyde, offered free use of the property for the duration of the war and for a dozen years after the declaration of peace. It had sat empty for around sixteen years. He also gave the option to make the institution a permanent one on payment of the agricultural value of the ground. John Reid bought the house and grounds and presented them to the hospital.

In addition to money from the public to help with the project, gifts in kind were donated. An operating theatre and dispensary were fitted out and another dispensary created.

In little more than twelve months, the hospital had treated more than 1500 patients. Additional temporary accommodation was built to cater for the demand and took the total number of beds to 400 on the site.

Once the Princess Louise was functional, one in five of the disabled British veterans from the First World War was treated at Erskine. There was a terrible shortage of artificial limbs at the time, a problem created by the huge number of amputees returning from the continent. Sir William Macewen, the respected surgeon leading the Erskine team at the time, responded by calling in the help of the Clydeside shipyard workers. The Erskine limb was devised, and thousands were fitted after being carefully crafted both in the shipyards and in the workshops that had sprung up at the hospital. By the end of 1920 more than 9,500 artificial limbs had been fitted.

Today technology has moved on, but the demands on the services of the charity remain great. Through the Falklands, the Gulf War, Bosnia, Northern Ireland, Afghanistan and Iraq the British armed forces have fought and have sustained casualties.

Erskine has kept pace. In the 1950s the original hospital was modernised with the addition of a new block to deal with acute medical cases, replacing the old First World War huts that had been hastily installed. In the 1960s a further four large wards were added in a major extension. In the 1980s the aim was consolidation as the old mansion house began to suffer from dry rot and other vagaries of age, leading to greater thought towards the long-term future for Erskine. In 2000 the new purpose-built home was opened to residents.

Erskine continues to look to the future and has developed an innovative schools programme designed to educate the next generation about the sacrifices and experiences of the country's service personnel. The pack created by the charity includes the recollections of a number of veterans bringing history to life in the most vivid fashion and helping to forge links with the next generation.

Education is one aspect and brand awareness another as the charity bids to continue its lifeline fundraising drive. Each year Erskine Week commemorates the anniversary of the official opening of the original hospital, which took place in June 1967. By then hundreds of soldiers had already been sent to the facility for treatment. Erskine Week brings a series of events designed to raise awareness and funds for Erskine as they support the 1,370 former servicemen and women who come under their care.

While the money raised by the Rangers Supporters Erskine Appeal has been hugely beneficial in meeting that aim, Erskine also benefits from donations of an equally precious commodity

– time. The charity welcomes volunteers in a whole host of roles, with everything from office administration and library duties to assisting with care in a variety of ways. Volunteers range from teenagers right through the age spectrum, and many have had their efforts rewarded through schemes such as the Duke of Edinburgh Award and Queen's Badge.

Erskine also runs an employment programme, with four commercial enterprises based at Bishopton which employ former service personnel and disabled workers. Erskine Print and Erskine Furniture sit along with the site's garden centre and coffee shop, as well as the Reid Macewen training and conference centre to add another few strings to the organisation's bow. It is all part of the strategy to provide all-encompassing care and support for veterans in a variety of stages of life and with very different needs. Everyone is part of the Erskine family and the spirit fostered by the body has earned huge praise from various inspection authorities.

It is that attention to care that has brought such strong support from so many quarters. Rangers are not the only club to have taken to the Erskine cause. Hearts, with their proud military heritage, have also been very active fundraisers for a number of years and have been at the forefront of promoting the work of the charity and other forces' causes.

The Bears have also developed a proud tradition of supporting veteran soldiers – and the warmth extended to Britain's troops has extended far beyond that. The club has thrown open its doors to hundreds of current troops in recent years in recognition of their service in modern combat zones, including Afghanistan.

As the championship was being won in the closing weeks of the 2010/11 season, more than 100 members of the 2 Scots Regiment travelled to Ibrox to cheer on the Light Blues against Hearts. It was a welcome period of rest and relaxation after six gruelling months of service in Afghanistan, where the Penicuik-based soldiers had been providing security in Helmand Province at Lashkar Gah City.

At the time of the visit, Walter Smith remarked: 'Footballers are regarded as heroes, but the men and women who are fighting for their country on the frontline are the true heroes in life.'

True to form, the Rangers support gave the troops a rapturous welcome. Earlier in the season, in November 2010, Ibrox had been turned into a sea of red and white with a card display covering all corners of the Ibrox stands depicting a series of poppies to mark remembrance weekend. A group of 120 Royal Navy personnel were in the crowd that day, with the Rangers players proudly wearing the poppy on the light blue shirts, and thousands of pounds were raised for Poppy Scotland.

Other regiments to have been entertained at Ibrox include the Argyll and Sutherland Highlanders, 5th Battalion, The Royal Regiment of Scotland and the Royal Marines from 45 Commando. In 2009 there were 1,000 troops in the ground for the European tie against Unirea Urziceni.

The club also joined the Tickets for Troops scheme in 2009 and within a year had donated more than 3,000 tickets for the benefit of servicemen and women in the British forces. Musical venues, theatres and other sports arenas also signed up and provided tickets for more than 70,000 troops who registered.

In 2009 the True Colours initiative was launched by the Rangers Supporters Assembly, designed to encourage fans to buy season tickets and to consider the potential for donating that seat to a fan from the forces, or to give up the ticket on a match-by-match basis to be used by men and women from the services. Later that summer the first team squad took time out from pre-season training in Germany, during the pre-season camp on the continent, to meet British troops stationed nearby.

The support for Erskine has been unbending and the efforts have not gone unnoticed by an appreciative board of trustees. The harsh realities for the charity, however, suggest that fundraising will have to continue at the same rate as in previous years to help maintain the level of care being provided for Scotland's veterans.

Chief executive Major Jim Panton and chairman Jim Scott stated in their latest annual report:

There is no doubt that 2010 was a great year for Erskine. Those who have followed and supported us will remember the Erskine 2010 Appeal in the late 1990s, and the associated objectives which set out an ambitious plan to modernise and expand the organisation.

Visitors to Erskine today acknowledge an exceptional job when they see how the strategy, first set out in 1996, has transformed our charity into a modern day, state-of-the-art care provider for the Armed Forces community.

In the last year alone there has been an enormous amount of positive stories, developments, events and activities that, combined, support the claims we make about the overall capability of Erskine today. As in previous years, the overall impact of Erskine in 2010 would never have been possible without the loyal band of Erskine supporters from all walks of life, who have once again shown their deep appreciation for the men and women of our Armed Forces by supporting Erskine's efforts with much needed funds.

While reflecting on the significant progress Erskine has made in the last ten to fifteen years, 2010 was the year where we turned our attention to the future. Once again we were faced with asking the same deep question about future requirements that we asked in 1996; what will the support requirements be in ten to fifteen years and what do we need to do now to get ready for that?

We have started reorganising the charity with a new executive management team structure and adjustments to our trustee governance structure. The new strategy, which will focus our efforts up to our 100th birthday in October 2016, has begun.

We have made historic changes to our admissions policy for residential care, as we begin to anticipate the future demographic changes in our beneficiary groups. At the same time our work in partnership with the Ministry of Defence and other service charities, supporting those injured in Iraq and Afghanistan, continues to develop and a new contract extends the Personnel Recovery Centre at Erskine Edinburgh for another two years.

So, why begin an era of change so soon? Why don't we simply settle with the extremely positive and satisfactory set-up we have across our range of activities and locations? As costs continue to grow, in line with current budgets, income is not keeping up as the fundraising environment changes and the wider economic recession begins to bite further into our different income streams.

Therefore, we face the same challenge we faced in the mid-1990s. From a position of current strength, we need to combine a well-educated prediction of future need and the services that will be required to best meet that need. The harsh reality is our current financial trajectory could put us in difficulty in five to ten years time unless we begin a steady set of corrective actions now. All that said, there is much to be very positive about. Erskine has achieved an immense amount historically and in recent years. All who have been part of that deserve to be very proud of their contribution.

Above all, Erskine now has a significant opportunity to be amongst the first to prepare for the future needs of those we will be called on to support, and to lead others in developing effective ways of doing that. The future is looking challenging, but extremely bright for Erskine.

With the weight of the Rangers family well and truly behind them, the efforts to keep the pounds rolling in for Erskine show no sign of abating as the memory of what servicemen and women of all eras have done for Britain remains prominent in the minds of hundreds of thousands of Gers fans.